ALSO BY I.V. HILLIARD

Experiencing The Fresh Fire Anointing

Mental Toughness for Success

Men @ Work

Living The Maximized Life

Secrets To A Better Life

10 Mistakes Most Failures Make

The Hidden Light

The Cup, THE CAKE & THE COIN

Keys To Honoring Spiritual Leadership

DR I.V. HILLIARD

New Spectrum Media Concepts

HOUSTON

Unless marked, all Scripture quotations are taken from the King James Version. (KJV) Scripture quotations marked AMP are taken from the Amplified® Bible, Copyright © 1954, 1958, 1962, 1964, 1965, 1987 by The Lockman Foundation. Used by permission.

Emphasis within Scripture quotations is the author's own. Please note that New Spectrum Media Concepts' style capitalizes all pronouns in Scripture that refer to God. The name satan and related references are not capitalized intentionally.

This book is protected by the copyright laws of the United States of America. This book may not be copied or reprinted for commercial gain or profit. No part of this publication may be reproduced, distributed, or transmitted in any form or by any means or stored in a database or retrieval system without prior written permission of the Publisher.

The use of short quotations or occasional page copying for personal or group study is permitted and encouraged. Permission will be granted upon request.

The Cup, The Cake and The Coin:
Keys to Honoring Spiritual Leadership
Copyright © 2012 New Spectrum Media Concepts
ISBN 13: 978-0-9851176-0-3

Published by New Spectrum Media Concepts
15814 Champions Forest #75
Spring, TX 77379
www.newspectrummedia.com

Dedication & Acknowledgements

I have often said, we are the sum total of what others have deposited into our lives that we choose to accept. Through the course of my 50 years in ministry, as I reflect on the impact the many spiritual leaders that God has brought into my life, I am amazed at the diversity of the men and women of God from whom I have gleaned. I am eternally grateful for the deposits each of them made in my life and to list everyone of them would be a book in itself.

I do, however, want to acknowledge a few of them; and, even though some of them have been received in Heaven, the impact and their deposit in my life was not in vain. My natural father Theodore Hilliard told me some thing years ago that made an impression on my life that I carry to this day. My dad said to me, "There will be many people that will come into your life so do not waste their time."

From each one of these great men of God I have received and applied different aspects of their investment in my life. Publicly and privately, I have told them how much I appreciate their investment.

I received my call to preach the gospel at the age of 9 years old and my Mother took me to our Pastor, Rev. N. T. Burks. Week after week, he made an investment in my life by teaching me to value the art of studying the Word of God. It was his sage wisdom that I needed. He offered my mother wisdom to allow me to grow up as a normal boy and not treat me any differently because I was called to preach. Today, his voice of wisdom still guides me in my study and the preparation of my messages.

Later in my teenage life, my Mother took me to Rev. O. C. Johnson, who served as the Pastor of the Lyons Unity Missionary Baptist Church for over 35 years. It is through his life that I saw humility and learned many of the principles I share in this book. I came to know Rev. C. L. Jackson at one of the most crucial times in my ministry. Much like the people that were rope holders for the Apostle Paul, Rev C. L. Jackson held the rope for me and taught me the boldness to obey God regardless of opposition.

Through the years of obeying God and carrying out my pastoral assignment, I was connected with Rev. A.L. Patterson who I acknowledge as the one who has mastered the art of homiletics and alliteration. His example has given me 'joy for my journey' as a teacher.

Years ago, I was impacted by the life of Rev. E. V. Hill. During his life, I was allowed to work for him through a soul-winning outreach program he started. I was impacted by his administrative skills and the power of delegation. He was involved in many spheres of church, community and business yet he was able to do them all with ease because he was a prolific delegator. Apostle Frederick K. C. Price transformed my life and ministry with his discipline to live by faith.

Through his example and teaching, I came to understand how to effectively communicate the faith message.

A few years ago, God said that He would "give me sons and daughters like unto myself." I have seen this manifest in an overwhelming manner as they have set a new standard of generosity in the Body of Christ by serving, praying and sowing into Pastor Bridget's and my life. I dedicate this book to all of them.

I thank God that I learned years ago, that when your heart is right towards God and your desire is to please Him then He is obligated to bring you into the company of the people you need to know and the knowledge of the things you need to know that are critical for your success and destiny in life. I can honestly say that God has definitely caused me to be brought into the company of many great men and women of God so whether their name is listed above or not, I acknowledge their impact on my life and I honor them for all that they did for me and others in the kingdom of God.

Table Of Contents

Dedication & Acknowledgements — vii

Introduction — 1

The Controversial Concern - The Resistance — 21

The Conscious Choice - The Revelation — 55

The Criteria Component - The Recognition — 87

The Character Correction - The Renegades — 105

The Corporate Commitment - The Responsibility — 127

The Compassionate Choice - The Restoration — 145

Epilogue — 169

Introduction

WHY WRITE THIS BOOK

You have in your hands a book, which I believe God has mandated that I write! There is a Biblical truth that has been overlooked or not taught with conviction; and thus, today, there is a generation who has not tapped into the supernatural provisions of God. This principle is one that I learned and embraced over four decades ago. My wife and I are living examples that this Biblical practice works. Whenever I am asked about church management or leadership, before too long, the discussion turns to the compensation of spiritual leaders. The Spirit of God has assigned me to document this revelation and make it available to all those seeking to please God by honoring Spiritual Leadership. The Spirit of God would not have me write this book without already having prepared the hearts of millions to receive this revelation and immediately put it into practice. Let me start by giving you my story!

In the early 70's, I made an unwise decision that derailed my pathway to success. Having finished high school in the upper part of my class, I was on the track to become a Chemical Engineer. As is usually the case with high performing students, offers came pouring in. I was sought out by Shell Oil Company and placed in their engineer development program, which guaranteed me a job as a Chemical Engineer upon completion of the Bachelor's of Science program at the University of Texas. I was on my way!! I was enrolled in school and could see nothing but bright skies and sunny days ahead. Then, I thought I was in love! I fell hard and no longer was school or the internship on my mind. I wanted to be married. As a result, I forfeited the four-year scholarship to the University of Texas and the work-study program with Shell Oil Company.

It was a tragic move that everyone in my life tried to talk me out of, except, of course, my fiancé. Obviously, I did not value the opportunity that I had been so fortunate to receive. These were the early 70's and during that time, opportunities for young black men were very limited. I was in an advantaged place and didn't value it. I vividly recall my father pleading with me to stay in college while attempting to persuade me that marriage could wait. Unfortunately, the impetuousness of youth took over, and I rejected every effort he made to dissuade me.

I withdrew from school and started a family. I had saved some money from the work-study program that I redirected to setting up house, but it didn't go far at all. Reality set in and I knew I needed to secure real work. Well, reality set in as I could only find a job paying a little above minimum wage in a hardware supply company. It was then when I realized that I had blown it! The little salary that I was making was nothing like the excessive pay I was getting from the work-study program. You see, Shell Oil's work-study compensation plan was designed to afford the students the opportunity to purchase clothing for school, books, and even pay tuition. This was like a full scholarship with the provision that I had to work for the company over the summer months. Mistakenly, I thought that since it was what I was worth to Shell, another company would see my value as well. I made a serious miscalculation.

As I settled into this new life of lack and struggle, I was very depressed. I was married with a child on the way and working in a dead end job making a little above minimum wage. Needless to say, there were no fringe benefits and I owed every cent of my paycheck before payday arrived. Things were so bad financially that I could not even meet the job safety requirement of owning steel-toe boots. Against policy, I purchased the imitation steel-toe boots, which had extra layers of leather where the steel should have been. Times were bad and the outlook was even worse. Life was hard and payday was depressing.

I could not see any way out; I was in a hopeless situation, barely making it from week to week. Housing for my little family and me was even more depressing. I could only afford an apartment that was just above the government subsidized housing. In fact, the complex, where I lived, had served as the overflow for the government housing project. When tenants were waiting for permanent housing in the projects, they were placed in this apartment complex until their apartments were ready. So, this was a transient, bug-infested place that I was ashamed of, but I couldn't do any better. If ever there were a hog pen experience like the prodigal son experienced, this was it! I say so often, now in retrospect, what you will not learn from the wisdom of others, the hog pen will make crystal clear. To me, it was clear that I had blown it; I had made a serious mistake in judgment and had derailed my life and future.

I was on the brink of serious depression. The only relief I had was on Sunday while attending the Baptist Church where I grew up. It was there when I enjoyed a time of spiritual refreshing. I was an associate minister at the church and my Pastor really loved me. He saw the condition I had gotten myself in and from time to time he would allow me to preach; and, my how I looked forward to those times. Not just for the small honorarium that was given, but it gave me a chance to do what I loved to do, which is to preach the Gospel. I had accepted the call to preach as a nine-year old child, after I received a visitation from an angel. I preached my first sermon at ten years old, and by the time, all of this drama was happening in my life, I had been preaching several years.

Everyone around me knew of my plight and felt sorry for me but to no avail. Most of those I knew could not help me because they were barely surviving too. I prayed and asked God to help me, but I did not know how the help would come. I thought about going back to school but on my salary that was out of the question. Life was hard and getting harder! Money was tight and getting tighter! There seemed to be no way out of the rut that I had acquired.

Even as I write about it today, I can identify with the sense of hopelessness and helplessness I experienced during those times. I understand why people in seemingly hopeless states are driven to crime, drugs, abandonment, and even suicide. I know what it feels like to see a dream become a nightmare from which you seemingly cannot awaken. I know what it feels like to think about ending it all because you had so much promise and you just blew it. I know what it feels like to carry the shame of a foolish mistake, have people look at you, and quickly look away in disgust and shame.

Well, it's a long way from those days to where I am today. Thank God, that He will not leave us in our bleak situations even when they are of our own making.

My breakthrough came when a man approached me, one day, and said, "Ira, the Bible says that God will bless you if you will tithe." Then, and I still can't believe this, the next words he spoke were, "But, now I'm not a tither." Can you believe that? He was telling me about doing something that he was not doing himself. I was neither offended nor was I going to discount what he said. Ever since I gave my life to Christ, I have always sought to be sensitive to obey truth no matter where it came from. His words were like music to my ears. For the first time, someone told me something that I could do now to get God to help me in my situation.

Tithing! From time to time, I had heard about it by the preacher in church, but I had never studied it or fully understood all of its ramifications. Once this fellow told me about it, I could not shake it. I knew that tithing was giving a tenth of what I earned to God, and though my money was tighter than tight, I could not get this out of my mind. I know now, that it was the Holy Spirit tugging on me to position me into God's plan for my life.

That day, when I came home, I picked up my Bible and went through it while searching the Scriptural passages about tithing and giving offerings. After that evening of study, I was convinced that it was the plan of God for His covenant people to honor Him by giving tithes and offerings. I was persuaded of God's promise that He would get involved in their lives to bless them with favor and increase. I will cover the specific passages that I read back then, which thoroughly convicted and convinced me that my situation would change if I would become a giver of tithes and offerings.

Although my study was targeted at the tithe, I clearly saw that the famous third chapter of Malachi spoke of tithes and offerings. It did shake me a bit when I read that not only was God expecting me to give Him a tenth of what I earned as an act of obedience and honor, but He also required an offering. The part about the offering had interested me because I wanted to know what amount of offering would please God. I could see that the tithe was based on a percentage, but the offering was a different matter altogether. God left the amount of the offering up to the giver, and I saw that there were different types of blessings attached to different types of offerings.

It was during this time of study that I discovered the giving of my offering to honor Spiritual Leadership. I had never heard this before; it was right there in the Bible; and I had read this, but never saw it in this light. It was clear what God required, and would reward those who would give offerings to their Spiritual Leadership; in my case, it was my Pastor. At first, it was almost more than I could bear, because you see, I was only earning $65.00 per week before taxes at the warehouse job. I was already stretched thinner than thin, yet I could see that I owed God the tenth. Otherwise, I would be considered a God-robber and would continue to live under the curse. No person wants to live under a curse that is representative of God's disapproval.

This newfound knowledge called for a decision that I knew I had to make before the next payday. I prayed about it and asked God for strength to obey Him in this area. I was excited when I saw that the Scripture said I could prove Him in my finances. That's right; God said I could test this out. I decided to trust God and His Scriptural plan for my life by becoming a tither and a giver of offerings. The offering that most interested me was the offering that promised a return when you give to your Spiritual Leadership. Therefore, I decided that with the next payday, I would cash my check on Friday, set aside $6.50 for my tithes; and give $5.00 to my Pastor as an offering to honor and bless my Spiritual Leader.

Now, that may not look like much to you at this time, but for me, that was bountiful giving at the sacrificial level. I had creditors whom I had to renegotiate with; I had to refigure my budget, and I had to go without some things to keep this commitment. However, I was convinced that if I did so, I would be the better. Among other reasons, this book is written to chronicle for you what God has done for me, since I made that commitment to honor Him with the tithe and to honor spiritual leadership with offerings.

It was a refreshing week when I became a tither and gave that $5.00 offering to honor my man of God; I expected something good to happen. I remember the reluctance of my Pastor when I put the $5.00 bill in his hand. He looked at me with utter dismay and tried to give the money back to me. I remember him saying that he knew how tough things were for me and he could not take my money. I recalled that I insisted on him taking the offering, and told him how this offering was not about him, but about a principle I found in the Bible. I expressed to him that when applying this principle, my obedience to God would obligate God to bless me. This principle, which I began to practice that day, is the principle that the Holy Spirit has directed me to share with you in this book. As a result of my obedience, I really expected something good to happen in my life.

In addition to feeling really good about my commitment, nothing significant happened that first week. The next week when I was paid, I repeated the process by giving $6.50 to the church and $5.00 to honor my Pastor. This went on for several weeks, and my expectations for something good happening in my life had manifested about the third or fourth week. I will never forget this day!

I went to work as I normally did on that Thursday, as I recall. I was called into the upstairs management office. You see, I worked on the warehouse floor and the offices of the owner and management staff was upstairs. I hadn't been to the upstairs offices since the day I met with the bookkeeper, signed the employment forms and received company paperwork. Initially, I was a bit concerned because I thought that upper management had discovered that I did not own steel-toed boots (a violation of company policy). All kinds of thoughts rushed through my mind as I climbed the stairs to the Senior Manager's office.

I had only met him once during the interview process; he was kind, a tall, robust, mixed grey-headed fellow. All the workers said he had been a Sergeant in the Vietnam War and that he was stern and meant business. He was always nice to me, but why was I being called to his office? What had I done? What was about to happen to me? I could not afford to lose this job because it was difficult to find. I had undergone interview, after interview, after interview. I had finally landed this job. The last thing I wanted to do was to go job-hunting again. I didn't know whether I was perspiring from the walk up the stairs or from the fear attack, but I was finally at his open door.

To my surprise, he got up from his desk with a big grin on his face and walked toward me with an outstretched hand. We shook hands and he asked me to take a seat. Then, he began to tell me the reason for our impromptu meeting. He stated that my immediate supervisor had resigned and had recommended me to assume the supervisory role in the department. Wow! This was the last thing on my mind since I had the least seniority of all the workers in the department. Further, I did not have a relationship at all with the supervisor, other than I did my work with excellence. Assuming that I would accept the new position, the Senior Manager went on to tell me what my new salary would be; and though I had not seen the check, it was refreshing just to hear I was getting an increase. To my surprise, he told me that my new rate would be on my next check, which was the next day. Through the help of the Holy Spirit, the next thought that came to my mind was that my tithing and my giving was working and the blessings were manifesting.

The next Sunday was exciting because I could hardly wait for the offering time to give my increased tithes. After the service, I gave my increased honor offering to my Pastor. You should have seen the look on his face when I gave him his offering this time. I really don't remember the exact amount of the increased amount of my honor offering; but every time I received increase, I was faithful to the principle.

My testimony continues beyond this first increase. It gets better. Several weeks into my new position as supervisor, I had a creative idea to rearrange some things in the warehouse that saved the company a significant amount of money; and as a result, I was given another increase. Of course, you know that meant my tithing increased and my giving to my spiritual leader increased. For the first time things were really looking up; the financial pressure was not so great and more opportunities to preach were being received.

About three months into practicing these principles of tithing and giving to spiritual leadership, something monumental happened that was nothing short of a supernatural move of God. One day, while working in the warehouse, enjoying my new and increased financial position, a young Hispanic gentleman from another department approached me with a statement that stunned me. His name was Arnold Gonzales, and he said, "Ira, you are a mighty smart guy to be working in a place like this." I was stunned and replied with disdain, "Well, you work here too!" Arnold told me that he was working for the warehouse part-time, but his fulltime job was with a company called, Southwest Data Management, which was a computer company. Arnold was a computer operator and swore that he would tell the owner of the company about me.

To my surprise, the next day, Arnold came to my department with a big smile and handed me a business card from the president of Southwest Data Management, Frank Kurtin. Arnold recounted a conversation he had with Mr. Kurtin about me and said Mr. Kurtin wanted to talk to me. Arnold told me that

Southwest Data Management currently had no job openings; but Mr. Kurtin expressed a willingness to take my application and keep it on file for the time when a Computer Operator trainee opportunity surfaced in the future. As he gave me the business card, he stated that Mr. Kurtin was expecting me to call him.

Later that day, I made the call, spoke directly to Mr. Kurtin and what a refreshing call that was. He stated that there were no Job Openings at present, but Arnold had given me a raving recommendation that stirred his interest in me. Mr. Kurtin suggested that the next time I was in the area; I should stop by, complete an application, and be interviewed. I told him I would be there the next day. He sensed my eagerness; and, again, he told me that there were no present job openings and there was no sense of urgency. I convinced him that tomorrow was a good day for me and he agreed.

I could not articulate it then, but the favor of God had been released on my life. Now, others were going out of their way to use their power and influence to help me. I arrived about fifteen minutes before the appointment with Mr. Kurtin and noticed as I looked around; I would not need to wear working boots there. Everyone I saw was sharply dressed in business attire. This was the kind of dress attire that I was required to wear when I worked in the office of Shell Oil Company. My heart pounded within my chest as Mr. Kurtin's secretary called my name and said that he was ready to see me.

When I walked into his spacious office and began to dialogue with him, I knew this was a destiny moment for me. He began to recant that there were no job openings. As he glanced through the application that I had completed while waiting in the reception area, he asked me to follow him to another office. There he gave me the instructions for taking their Standard Aptitude Test. He presented the papers, set the timer, and walked out. I had not been in this type of classroom testing setting for quite some time and was not really expecting to take a test, but I was going to give this my best shot.

When the timer buzzer sounded, I had completed the test and had time to review several answers to some of the most difficult questions. I was confident that I had done my best. Mr. Kurtin took the completed test papers and told me to wait until he returned with the results. The minutes seemed like hours, but finally, when Mr. Kurtin burst through the door, I noticed he had a big smile on his face. Holding the papers in his hands like a torch, he declared, "This has never happened in the history of our company! You made a perfect score on this test. We don't have any job openings, but we are going to make one for you!"

Those words still resonate in me because this was the declaration of a career change and another opportunity to succeed. Again, my expectation of something good happening in my life were being fulfilled because I obeyed God in giving of my tithes and offerings. I knew this opportunity was given to me by divine orchestration and that the wind of divine favor was blowing on my sails. Mr. Kurtin discussed the employment particulars: the salary offer, which almost tripled what I was making at the time, the job duties, company benefits, and future opportunities. I returned to the warehouse, resigned, gave sufficient notice, and worked faithfully until I satisfied my obligations.

I still remember what my thoughts were on that very first day of the new job. I knew for certainty that my tithing and offerings to honor spiritual leadership had brought me to this place of divine favor. It was a liberating experience. I had the chance to learn new skills in an industry that had endless possibilities for advancement. And the pay was so much better than I had imagined was possible for me in such a short period of time. I was not bothered about the 90-day probationary period because I knew that I was well equipped to handle whatever was placed before me. The Aptitude test results encouraged me that I had the intellectual ability to do the job because I had scored higher than all the other Computer Operators that had been hired.

By this time, I had opened a checking account. As soon as I deposited my check, I could hardly wait to write out the check to my church for my tithes and to give my Pastor his love (honor) offering. I am committed to these principles for life because I practiced them long before I became a Pastor. I am not teaching this because I see a personal benefit for me. This gives me the undeniable credibility to write on this subject because I discovered and obeyed these principles at a time in my life when others would have said that I could not afford to give any money away, especially to the church.

The more I began to read about the blessing of God coming upon those who would honor their spiritual leader, in various ways; the more confidence I had in the pathway I had taken. I had decided that I would live a life, which God promised in the Scripture for those who obeyed these divine principles.

This book is so appropriately named, the cup, the cake, and the coin, because these are the instruments used in Scripture to bless and honor spiritual leadership. The action of blessing spiritual leadership seems to trigger an intervention of the power of God to rescue from problem situations. When looking through the pages of Scripture for validation of the premise of this book, several episodes surfaced that provide the three witnesses required to establish a spiritual claim. From the lips of the Lord Jesus Himself this idea of being rewarded for honoring spiritual leaders is established. Here in the pages of the Gospel is the promise of reward to those who bless the men and the women of God with as much as a cup of water.

> "He who receives and welcomes and accepts you receives and welcomes and accepts Me, and he who receives and welcomes and accepts Me receives and welcomes and accepts Him Who sent Me. He who receives and welcomes and accepts a prophet because he is a prophet shall receive a prophet's reward, and he who receives and welcomes and accepts a righteous man because he is a righteous man shall receive a righteous man's reward. And whoever gives to one of these little ones [in rank or influence] even a cup

> of cold water because he is My disciple, surely I declare to you, he shall not lose his reward."
> (Matthew 9:40-42 AMP)

It is exciting to know that not so much as a cup of water given to bless leadership will go unnoticed or unrewarded by the Father. The story of the widow sustaining the prophet with her last cake has been the poster story of the promised blessing that comes upon you for taking care of the spiritual leadership. Her willingness to trust the principle that is being outlined in this book is what positioned her for the miracle that saved her and her family.

> "And the Word of the LORD came unto him, saying, Arise, get thee to Zarephath, which belongeth to Zidon, and dwell there: behold, I have commanded a widow woman there to sustain thee. So he arose and went to Zarephath. And when he came to the gate of the city, behold, the widow woman was there gathering of sticks: and he called to her, and said, Fetch me, I pray thee, a little water in a vessel, that I may drink. And as she was going to fetch it, he called to her, and said, Bring me, I pray thee, a morsel of bread in thine hand. And she said, As the LORD thy God liveth, I have not a cake, but an handful of meal in a barrel, and a little oil in a cruse: and, behold, I am gathering two sticks, that I may go in and dress it for me and my son, that we may eat it, and die. And Elijah said unto her, Fear not;

> *go and do as thou hast said: but make me thereof a little cake first, and bring it unto me, and after make for thee and for thy son. For thus saith the LORD God of Israel, The barrel of meal shall not waste, neither shall the cruse of oil fail, until the day that the LORD sendeth rain upon the earth. And she went and did according to the saying of Elijah: and she, and he, and her house, did eat many days. And the barrel of meal wasted not, neither did the cruse of oil fail, according to the Word of the LORD, which he spake by Elijah." (1Kings 17:8-16)*

From reading the passage, it is clear to see that giving to your leader must be an act of faith with the expectation of a reward. The reason for this book is to teach you this principle and position you in a faith state of mind so that you can receive the supernatural return on your giving.

Finally, the day that Peter took upon himself to assist Jesus, his spiritual leader, in paying his temple tax, Peter acquired enough resources to pay his own debt. Giving financial support to those who are in spiritual leadership is referenced throughout the Scriptures. From the Old Testament record of the tithes and offerings being given to the priests, to the church at Philippi giving to the Apostle Paul, the Scripture bears record that God ordains such giving. When Peter accepted to help Jesus get the money to pay the temple tax, he probably had no idea that his efforts would trigger a blessing of what he needed. God will never allow us to do anything for Him for which He will not reward us.

> "When they arrived in Capernaum, the collectors of the half shekel [the temple tax] went up to Peter and said, Does not your Teacher pay the half shekel? He answered, Yes. And when he came home, Jesus spoke to him [about it] first, saying, What do you think, Simon? From whom do earthly rulers collect duties or tribute—from their own sons or from others not of their own family? And when Peter said, From other people not of their own family, Jesus said to him, Then the sons are exempt. However, in order not to give offense and cause them to stumble [that is, to cause them to judge unfavorably and unjustly] go down to the sea and throw in a hook. Take the first fish that comes up, and when you open its mouth you will find there a shekel. Take it and give it to them to pay the temple tax for Me and for yourself."
>
> (Matthew 17:24-27)

These stories and more will be addressed throughout this book to give you the supportive Scriptural evidence to prove this principle. My testimony is far too extensive to cover in this opening section. There is much more to my testimony that will be peppered throughout the pages of this book, which will provide a systematic plan of action for all who are serious about embracing this supernatural life. I have written this book to clear up the myths and show you the Scriptural order of God. To obey these principles, I am convinced that we do not need endorsement from the secular world. What will be presented in the following pages are spiritual principles, which the unbeliever cannot understand or aspire to without the mind of Christ.

So then, this book is not written to convince the critics or persuade the unbeliever, but to strengthen those who are seekers of truth for a Biblical pathway to change their situation in life. I make no apology for all the Scriptures that will be used in this discourse because the Scriptural texts that I will use in proper context will legitimize this presentation. I pray that because you are reading this book, you are interested in tapping into a divine plan that will enable you to live a supernatural life in Jesus Christ.

20 THE CUP, THE CAKE & THE COIN

SECTION ONE

The Controversial Concern - The Resistance

I am not hesitant to inform you that as we engage this topic of giving honor, respect, and tangible gifts to spiritual leadership, there are those who will resist it. However, resistance does not mean that the topic is neither Biblical nor near to the heart of God. It just means that the forces of human misunderstanding and demonic intrusion have blinded people to its truth. As you will continue to see, there is a plethora of Biblical precepts to support what I am presenting to you. Let me be clear, these truths are not confusing; they are controversial! In fact, you will notice that those spiritual disciplines, which bring the greatest honor to God and benefit to us as Believers, are universally rejected by the carnally minded and the traditional religiously inclined. As Christ-followers, we should recognize our uniqueness and rejoice that we have a more excellent way! If we can agree that the Bible is our only textbook and that its words are inspired and infallible, it will facilitate our discussion in the next several chapters.

"All Scripture is given by inspiration of God, and is profitable for doctrine, for reproof, for correction, for instruction in righteousness,

> *that the man of God may be complete, thoroughly equipped for every good work." (1 Timothy 3:16)*

Scripture is profitable for doctrine, which establishes the order of God. For reproof which is the pinpointing of error and for correction which is exposure to truth. All of these work together so that we might mature and do good work. Let's start by debunking the myths and misunderstandings about giving money into the work of God.

THE MYTHS & MISUNDERSTANDING OF HONOR

The world rejects these spiritual truths because according to Scripture, it cannot comprehend their spiritual significance. Paul understood this and instructed the church in Corinth to be on guard as they interacted with the carnally minded.

> *"But the natural, nonspiritual man does not accept or welcome or admit into his heart the gifts and teachings and revelations of the Spirit of God, for they are folly (meaningless nonsense) to him; and he is incapable of knowing them [of progressively recognizing, understanding, and becoming better acquainted with them] because they are spiritually discerned and estimated and appreciated."*
> *(1 Corinthians 2:14)*

The principles that you are being taught must be spiritually discerned and not carnally deduced. Most things that Believers do are considered nonsense to unbelievers. Yet, even though they are ill equipped to embrace Biblical truths, we often allow their rejection of Biblical truth to intimidate us from obeying God's clear, Scriptural prescriptions. As Believers who have been called out of the world's system, I often wonder why we would want to follow their ways. It really does not make sense! Yet, there are many plain Biblical truths that we castoff and reject because they are not socially accepted.

As you read this revelation, I want to challenge you to keep an open mind because, while it may seem strange and different to you, I will give you irrefutable Biblical evidence to support it. Then, you will have to make a decision as to whether you will obey God or seek to please people who are not God-conscience in this area.

Resistance does not only come from the world! It will also come from carnal church people who have placed religious practice and traditions above righteous principles. There are those in church leadership who have held membership for many years; they would rather embrace unrighteous causes and make political compromises, before they would encourage church members to give offerings to the pastor. I am certain that if you have been around the church for any period of time, you have heard the religious rhetoric that has enslaved churches for decades, "God you keep him humble and we'll keep him poor." Some use finances as a way to control those in Spiritual leadership. Can you see how this mindset is a perversion of the Biblical truth that I seek to present?

God wants you to use your financial resources to bless His servant for several reasons. In the pages to come, you will see that this principle is God's method of sustaining those whom He calls into ministry. In addition, it is God's plan to bless you by rewarding your obedience with an impartation of divine favor, which brings increase to you. The carnal thinking of people has contaminated this process so that it is about manipulation and abuse. This is why so many churches struggle to move forward, expand, and make significant impact. You cannot disrespect God's servant and expect God's Spirit to move. One cancels out the other I believe this is why God has mandated that I share this truth with the Body of Christ. With the outpouring that God wants to release in the earth, it will not happen as long as His servants are undervalued and dishonored.

While many in our culture cannot quote Bible verses with ease, here is one universal adage that seems to be known by everyone: "All the preacher wants is your money." People can recite this with passion, whether they faithfully attended church or never darkened the threshold of the church. I find it simply amazing that in no other sector of society is this statement used, though it is blatantly true for those industries. For instance, what does your mortgage company want? Do they care that you stay in the home where you raised your children? Do they care that precious family pets are buried within its borders? No, if you do not pay your mortgage, they will take your home because all they want is your money.

When you go to the mall and walk into a store, though the sales person may flatter you with how good the clothes look on you and how those you respect will admire you, all they really want is your money! When the utility bill is due, do they care that you love Jesus? Do they care that you have little children who need electricity and gas? They could care less because all the utility company wants is your money! I could go on pointing out the absurdity of that statement and its inapplicability to your relationship with your man or woman of God.

By definition, money is a medium of exchange. You trade it for products and services. Economies operate that way. Also, it is used as a method of exchange in spiritual things, except God's servant who wants something greater than to receive your money. You will learn more about this later. However, know of a certainty that a real man or woman of God has a greater priority than your money! They want you to experience the blessing of God through your obedience to divine order. Unfortunately, because of the extreme controversy surrounding this type of giving, many ministers will not teach or preach on this subject. It is sad that it goes untapped and His people have no faith for what God has designed to do for them through these principles. It is my desire that others will learn this Scriptural principle and fervently, aggressively practice it! Your blessing will only manifest through consistently practicing what I am teaching you in this book.

There are many other myths and misunderstandings that handicap people from embracing this revelation; but as we journey together, you will see that honoring God's servant with your financial offerings are most Scriptural and pleases God!

THE MANIPULATIVE EXPLOITS OF THOSE HONORED

Let's be honest! Not every preacher who masquerades as a servant of the Most High is authentic! This should not be a discouragement to you in operating this principle. It should make you very discerning, so that you position yourself to receive the maximum return on the seed you sow into your man or woman of God.

There are charlatans who exploit God's people for their own selfish gain. The Bible is not silent about the fact that there will be people who misuse their office for their own profit. These people are easy to spot because they are quick to manufacture new gimmicks and schemes to persuade you to give.

> "If anyone teaches otherwise and does not consent to wholesome words, even the words of our Lord Jesus Christ, and to the doctrine which accords with godliness, he is proud, knowing nothing, but is obsessed with disputes and arguments over words, from which come envy, strife, reviling, evil suspicions, useless wranglings of men of corrupt minds and destitute of the truth, who suppose that godliness is a means of gain. From such withdraw yourself." (1 Timothy 6:3-5)

This passage instructs the believer to be discerning and to withdraw themselves from those who do such things. These preachers will misrepresent Scripture and manufacture revelation to extract resources from God's people. You should always be cautious as you hear appeals for support to ensure that you are sensing the leading of the Spirit of God and not being manipulated by a smooth talker.

In addition, there are those who exploit God's people for their own supremacy goals. Unfortunately, some enter the field of ministry because they desire to control and abuse people through the exercise of fraudulent spiritual authority. These fraudulent people seek to control every aspect of their congregant's life and family. Cults are often formed using these ungodly practices. Jesus expressly forbids this!

> "But Jesus called them to Himself and said, 'You know that the rulers of the Gentiles lord it over them, and those who are great exercise authority over them. Yet it shall not be so among you; but whoever desires to become great among you, let him be your servant.' "
> (Matthew 20:25-26)

True men and women of God are servants and have a servant's heart. They are sensitive about how to exercise spiritual authority like Jesus did. True shepherds are overseers of God's flock; they never seek to fleece them "as being lords over those entrusted to" them, "but being examples to the flock." (1 Peter 5:3)

You may also encounter those in ministry who exploit God's people as a sinful game. They will live openly, immoral lives and make spiritual excuses for their moral failings. A pastor is not perfect, but there is not one, shepherd or sheep, whom should tolerate blatant, unashamed display of sinful behavior. You may not be aware of this but you do not have to fall to sin.

> "Wherefore the rather, brethren, give diligence to make your calling and election sure: for if ye do these things, ye shall never fall."
> (1 Peter 1:10)

Leaders, just like people will be tempted to sin; but you do not have to fall to it. I am seeing a disturbing trend; Ministers openly commit sin and continue forward without any discipline, correction, or repentance. This sends the wrong signal about godly standards for leadership and the people of God. Be careful of those who equivocate with sin, make repeated calls to recognize their humanity, and that everyone sins! These are often telltale signs of open, unrepented sin. To those who would live these types of lifestyles, Jesus is very clear: "In the meantime, when an innumerable multitude of people had gathered together, so that they trampled one another, He began to say to His disciples first of all, 'Beware of the leaven of the Pharisees, which is hypocrisy. For there is nothing covered that will not be revealed, nor hidden that will not be known.' " (Luke 12:1-2) God will expose those who are playing this sinful game of hypocrisy and manipulation because He will not be mocked!

There are dishonest people who have ascended to the office of a pastor and their unholy behavior is obvious. Still, there are others who were never called to pastoral leadership but because of career limitations or the prompting of others, stepped out to lead a church. I am very much aware that not every person who heads a church is the model for a Biblical pastor. However, what I seek to explain to you through these pages is that you cannot suspend Scriptural principles, because some pastors do not exemplify Scriptural standards.

I really need you to hear my heart as I write about this. More God-called, God-consecrated, and God-committed men and women lead churches than those I previously described. Most pastors do not start out with ill motives, even though some do. Also, this is why you should stay ever vigilant to pray for your pastor "… that utterance may be given …" and that with boldness they "make known the mystery of the Gospel." (Ephesians 6:19) After almost 5 decades of ministry, I can tell you that your prayers are not only necessary; they are appreciated!

No doubt, you have encountered a pastor like the one I have previously described. This is not rationale for you to ignore God's instructions about the care of those pastors and leaders who are living righteous godly lives. If you have undeniable proof that your spiritual leader is in blatant violation and of righteous principles of Scripture and are unrepentant, you have justifiable grounds to leave that ministry and find another.

Think of it this way; have you ever had a bad experience at a restaurant? Did you stop eating in restaurants because of that one bad experience? Of course not! How about in the political arena? Have you known a politician who made promises and then broke them? Do you give up on all politicians because of the actions of one? Certainly not! How about teachers? Did you encounter a teacher who, try as she may, could not convey the subject matter and you were left more confused than ever? Did you give up on education? Absolutely not! Moreover, no leader is perfect nor does God require perfection, but He does require that the leader's heart be sold out on pleasing Him.

> *"The LORD has sought for Himself a man after His own heart, and the LORD has commanded him to be commander over His people."*
> *(1 Samuel 13:14)*

God wants a heart that is tender towards Him and His people.

Now, these may seem like trite questions but I want to illustrate a point. In other fields, we are prepared to handle the disappointments that occur and move forward. Yet, when it comes to pastors, we reject the pastor that disappointed us and all pastors, that church and all churches. Do you see the subtle strategy of the devil to steal a vital God-ordained relationship from you?

If you do not respect this principle, the devil knows that your next level blessing will be forfeited, which is tied to your man or woman of God. Guard that relationship and do not let it become corrupted by painting all pastors with the same brush.

In a later chapter, I will give you the specific criteria that will qualify pastors for honor. Here is a quick rubric to evaluate one worthy of your precious seed-faith offerings. Do they demonstrate that they love you? Do they teach you the Word of God? Do they model the Word of God before you? If the answer is "Yes," then, your pastor is probably good ground in which to sow.

THE MANDATE ESTABLISHING HONOR

We have already seen that pastors are God's servants and the Bible establishes the standard of care that they deserve.

> "Let him that is taught in the Word communicate unto him that teacheth in all good things." (Galatians 6:6)

That word, "communicate" means to provide financial support. Look at how this reads in the Amplified translation.

> "Let him who receives instruction in the Word [of God] share all good things with his teacher [contributing to his support]." (Galatians 6:6)

Thus, showing tangible honor to Spiritual leadership is not

only right; Scripture recommends it.

> "Let the elders that rule well be counted worthy of double honour, especially they who labour in the word and doctrine. For the Scripture saith, 'Thou shalt not muzzle the ox that treadeth out the corn. And, The labourer is worthy of his reward.' " (1 Timothy 5:17-18 NLT)

A church that does not honor its spiritual leadership is by Biblical standards an inferior church. Paul, whose credentials as a servant of God are undeniable, had a very interesting dialogue with the Church in Corinth. There were some questions as to whether or not Paul was deserving of financial support. Members of the Corinthian Church felt that they had no responsibility for sustaining Paul's preaching ministry. To their objections, Paul, in his inimical style, answers their questions with some pointed questions of his own.

> "Am I not an apostle? am I not free? have I not seen Jesus Christ our Lord? are not ye my work in the Lord? If I be not an apostle unto others, yet doubtless I am to you: for the seal of mine apostleship are ye in the Lord. Mine answer to them that do examine me is this, Have we not power to eat and to drink? Have we not power to lead about a sister, a wife, as well as other apostles, and as the brethren of the Lord, and Cephas? Or I only and Barnabas, have not we power to forbear working?

> Who goeth a warfare any time at his own charges? who planteth a vineyard, and eateth not of the fruit thereof? or who feedeth a flock, and eateth not of the milk of the flock?" (1 Corinthians 9:1-7)

Paul used Scripture as well as natural examples to explain why he was worthy of their financial support. Though Paul's argument was Scripturally sound and socially accurate, he released the Corinthian church from their financial responsibility for his care.

> "If others be partakers of this power over you, are not we rather? Nevertheless we have not used this power; but suffer all things, lest we should hinder the Gospel of Christ." (1 Corinthians 9:12)

Paul had a true pastor's heart because he saw that some of them struggled with the Biblical mandate to support God's servants. In order that he would not be a hindrance to their growth, he released them from supporting him financially. Yes, that's right he did so, but mistakenly, because in his next letter to this church he wrote to request their forgiveness. He states as you are about to read that their lack of financially supporting him caused them to be an inferior church.

Later, in 2 Corinthians, Paul writes them to revisit the issue.

> "Truly the signs of an apostle were wrought among you in all patience, in signs, and wonders, and

> mighty deeds. For what is it wherein ye were inferior to other churches, except it be that I myself was not burdensome to you? forgive me this wrong."
> (2 Corinthians 12:12-13)

This is incredible! Paul asked the Corinthian church to forgive him because in his desire not to offend them with a Biblical truth, he allowed them to become inferior! Only an inferior church would allow a man or woman of God to faithfully serve in teaching, praying, and serving and go unremunerated.

I remember how this truth became revolutionary in my thinking. Even though I had practiced the principle personally before I became a Pastor after becoming a Pastor, I would not allow my young church to give to me. Our church was small, resources low and I would sacrifice my salary week after week, thinking I was doing the right thing. What I did not realize was that I was causing my church to be an inferior church.

I remember seeking wisdom for my struggling ministry from a most successful Pastor in our city, Dr. C. L. Jackson. After explaining my lack of growth and failure in ministry, he asked about what support I was receiving from my church. Expecting to receive accolades from him for my noble sacrifices, I proudly told him I was not receiving a salary. What I received from him was a shockingly stern rebuke. He had me read out loud, 1 Corinthians 12:13-14. He quickly gave me revelation that I was robbing our church of its supernatural edge because I would not receive from them.

I repented and from that day to this day, I have unashamedly received financial support from the churches that I have served as Pastor. In fact, my support comes from a salary that is solely based on what is given by the members to finance pastoral support. So, what I have acquired over the last 30 years of ministry is what people have desired to give to me over the years.

Over the years, I have taught young pastors who have come to me with the same mindset I had years ago, and I shared the same principle that Dr. Jackson shared that day with me. It is an incredible defining moment with them, as it was with me, when I show them this supernatural principle. As I will show you in Scripture this is an ordained principle of God and should not be compromised under any circumstances.

Even though there are external pressures that keep pastors silent about teaching their members to show honor to spiritual leadership by giving them money, I am under a mandate from God to plainly reveal it so that its truth is undeniable and its benefits unmistakable!

I often hear Believers quote Philippians 4:19, which says, "… My God shall supply all your need according to his riches in glory by Christ Jesus."

However, this is not a general promise to be claimed. It is a specific reward or benefit that is granted to those who faithfully support spiritual leadership.

> "But it was right and commendable and noble of you to contribute for my needs and to share my difficulties with me. And you Philippians yourselves well know that in the early days of the Gospel ministry, when I left Macedonia, no church (assembly) entered into partnership with me and opened up [a debit and credit] account in giving and receiving except you only. For even in Thessalonica you sent [me contributions] for my needs, not only once but a second time."
> (Philippians 4:15-16 AMP)

Paul commended the Philippians for their generosity in supporting him financially. But, the return on the money that you give to your pastor is not just a financial one. The seed that you sow will produce a quality life. I like to call this a first-class lifestyle. One criticism that is levied against those who teach this is that they are manipulating people. (This is why I love God's Word because it answers our objections even before we raise them!)

> "Not because I desire a gift: but I desire fruit that may abound to your account. But I have all, and abound: I am full, having received of Epaphroditus the things which were sent from you, an odour of a sweet smell, a sacrifice acceptable, wellpleasing to God." (Philippians 4:17)

It is amazing that God considers your support to your spiritual leader (pastor) as a spiritual sacrifice, which He accepts and He is most pleased. When you give to those in spiritual leadership, it becomes a spiritual transaction of the highest order and it gets God's attention.

Honoring the man or woman of God with tangible gifts was not only a New Testament practice. It was an established order that the prophets and priests were supported by the special gifts brought to the tabernacle or temple. God wrote it into the offering system that a portion of what was brought went to undergird His servants. Moreover, when a person approached a spiritual leader for counsel, a gift was brought!

> "And he said unto him, Behold now, there is in this city a man of God, and he is an honourable man; all that he saith cometh surely to pass: now let us go thither; peradventure he can shew us our way that we should go. Then said Saul to his servant, But, behold, if we go, what shall we bring the man? for the bread is spent in our vessels, and there is not a present to bring to the man of God: what have we? And the servant answered Saul again, and said, Behold, I have here at hand the fourth part of a shekel of silver: that will I give to the man of God, to tell us our way." (1 Samuel 9:6-8)

This was a common practice in ancient days, which Saul fully respected. In doing so, he received prophetic counsel for his life and career that accelerated him along his path of destiny. This was not an attempt to purchase wisdom or buy a prophetic word, but a simple act of honor and respect. It would be a mistake to take this passage to use to attempt to justify charging people for prophetic words.

You may be saying to yourself, "I thought honoring my pastor meant showing appreciation and regularly expressing gratitude for his or her impact on my life." You are correct, but not complete. To honor spiritual authority means more than saying, "Thank you." Honor, in the Biblical context, means to give fitting and due respect, recognition, and resources. Look at this passage that speaks of honoring God that is written in the book of Proverbs.

> "Honour the LORD with thy substance, and with the firstfruits of all thine increase: So shall thy barns be filled with plenty, and thy presses shall burst out with new wine." (Proverbs 3:9-10)

Fitting and due respect is shown when you regularly recall that your pastor is commissioned and consecrated by God to help you. Your pastor is a part of God's plan to prosper you. Because there is a formal role that your pastor plays in your life, you must guard against unrealistic expectations. Your pastor is never commissioned by God to be your friend nor should you become too familiar, so that you devalue their divine role in your life. You may never have a meal with your pastor or spend time at their house. Yet, you can and must show them the respect that their office requires.

Fitting and due recognition is given when you formally honor your pastor. This may be through a pastor's appreciation, founder's day, birthday, or an anniversary service. These days are used to allow the members of the church the opportunity to recognize the significant work of their pastor. These days are always welcomed and in keeping with the Biblical expectation that spiritual leadership be given tangible, visible support. Every church ought to have some date calendared to intentionally call the church together to appreciate their pastor. So much is said negatively and innuendos are hurled at those who serve God's people; it is always a blessing to recognize those who labor faithfully among you.

You give fitting and due resources by dedicating monetary gifts for your pastor. This need not wait until an annual observance. In fact, as you recall my testimony, I established a system that I would give regularly to my man of God. This was personal over and above what was given to him by the church. You should too. Set aside an offering of your choice for your pastor and watch what this will produce in your life. Even if there is no place on the offering envelope, be intentional about giving to your pastor as often as possible. Now, you may say, that you would expect a pastor to say this. However, if you remember, I learned and practiced this principle when I was not a pastor! When you have structured your life around the truth of God's Word, it does not change. (I tithed when I was not pastoring and I continue to tithe now that I am a Pastor. Truth does not change. Neither did this truth of giving money to my pastor change.)

When you set your heart to honor your man or woman of God, it is an expression of their divine calling, compensation, and care. You have seen from Scripture already, there is a unique, but important spiritual role that your pastor plays in your life. Your honor affirms that you are aware and appreciate this divine calling and the God who called him or her. God also has set the compensation order for His servants.

> "Say I these things as a man? or saith not the law the same also? For it is written in the law of Moses, Thou shalt not muzzle the mouth of the ox that treadeth out the corn. Doth God take care for oxen? Or saith he it altogether for our sakes? For our sakes, no doubt, this is written: that he that ploweth should plow in hope; and that he that thresheth in hope should be partaker of his hope. If we have sown unto you spiritual things, is it a great thing if we shall reap your carnal things?"
> (1 Corinthians 9:8-11)

In addition, God has set a standard of care. I mentioned earlier about how important your prayers are to those who care for you spiritually. If you read Paul's letters to the churches, he often calls upon them to pray for him. Since you know that your pastor has a divine role to play in your life, they are worthy of your prayers. You should also become partner with them. Whatever God has called them to do, you should see it as your calling too. In Acts 16:9-10, you will see a pattern for this level of care.

> "And a vision appeared to Paul in the night. A man of Macedonia stood and pleaded with him, saying, 'Come over to Macedonia and help us.' Now after he had seen the vision, immediately we sought to go to Macedonia, concluding that the Lord had called us to preach the Gospel to them."
> (Acts 16:9-10)

Paul saw the vision and the people adopted it as theirs. You should do the same with your pastor.

THE MALEVOLENT EMOTIONS TO HONORING

Giving to God and others can be an emotionally trying experience. You will be amazed at the plethora of emotions that can be associated with the giving episode. Some of these emotions are good and positively add to the experience, while on the other hand, some of the emotions are very negative. These negative emotions are used by the devil to sabotage the giving experiences and mandates outlined in the Scripture.

Emotions are neurological manifestations or signals triggered by what we think or perceive to be true based on our deep-seated beliefs. When properly understood, our emotions can be used to help us initiate specific positive responses that will direct our lives on the course we desire and will eliminate undesirable behavior.

If our beliefs are flawed because of inaccurate information on giving that we were told before we were exposed to the truth, we could have negative emotions about giving. Negative emotions are deep seated, and exploited by the devil to disrupt our obedience at a strategic point of implementation. If the devil can cause us to reject this revelation of honoring spiritual leadership, he can rob us of the first-class lifestyle that Jesus died to give us. If he cannot stop us from giving, then he will attempt to cause us to honor spiritual leadership as a ritual and not a spiritual process. When we do this, we forfeit the harvest that God has promised.

Emotional enemies are antagonistic to Scriptural revelation knowledge because emotionally there will be an internal struggle for obedience. Once you lock onto misinformation, your core belief system is established. Then, it makes it extremely difficult to receive accurate information due to the emotional roadblocks these enemy emotions produce.

Sadly, you may have already been taught that it was wrong to give money to your pastor. Even though you cannot support this Scripturally, it was the information you received first on this concept. I am thankful that God loved you enough to have me take the time to reduce this revelation to writing, so that you can read and re-read it until it becomes a revelation to you.

As with every spiritual endeavor, our flesh is an unwilling accomplice. As you learn more about this important principle, you will encounter internal resistance, which, if you are not careful, will hinder you from receiving what I am presenting to you. Here are some negative emotions that you should be on guard, as you attempt to embrace this giving.

FEAR

The most common emotion associated with giving is that of fear. The fear of irrecoverable loss and potential substantial lack can dominate the mind and corrupt the deliberation to give. When you are not fully persuaded that giving will cause increase, there is the possibility of the fear of lack invading your heart and mind.

The widow of Zarepheth is an example of this negative emotion. She was given a direct command from God that she should provide for the prophet. We do not know if God told her before the famine happened or in the midst of it. Yet, when the prophet arrives, it couldn't have come at a worse time in her life. All her resources were depleted except a little flour and oil. She was ready to eat her last meal and die. But, the prophet instructed her to make his cake first. She was overcome by fear. She had a choice to make about her future. Either she would operate in faith and trust what God had told her, or operate in fear and take her chances with the famine. The prophet saw that she was gripped with fear. And, he admonished her with the following words.

"Fear not; go and do as thou hast said: but make

> me thereof a little cake first, and bring it unto me, and after make for thee and for thy son. For thus saith the LORD God of Israel, The barrel of meal shall not waste, neither shall the cruse of oil fail, until the day that the LORD sendeth rain upon the earth." (1 Kings 17:13-14)

She overcame her emotional fears and everyone in her household was preserved. Are you plagued by the fear of being fleeced? Are you afraid that if you commit to regularly give an offering to your pastor, you won't have enough to handle your financial responsibilities? These are all expressions of fear. Right now, you must check that emotion of fear or you will not be able to practice the principle that will tap the supernatural help you need for success in life.

SHAME

The next intimidating emotion is that of shame, which paralyzes and leads to inaction. Normally, shame is the product of some sort of flawed comparison to establish worth and value. When the comparison is made, there is a sense of inadequacy and less than, which brings on the feeling of embarrassment and shame. The following story of the disciples gives insight into handling the emotional deficit of shame.

Jesus and His disciples were in the countryside and without warning or notice, a whole multitude of people thronged Him. They were hungry. Jesus inquired of His followers what they had to feed the crowd. One by one, the disciples chimed in with their questions about how to solve this food shortage. Philip spoke of the financial impossibility of feeding so many people. Andrew took inventory and saw that the only food they had was 5 loaves of bread and 2 fish. He, then exclaimed, "...what is this among so many" (John 6:9)? In the presence of Jesus, Andrew was ashamed of the meager resources they had. Philip and Andrew miscalculated that Jesus already had a plan because "...for He Himself knew what he would do." (John 6:6) Their emotional baggage of shame caused them to see insufficiency in the presence of the All-Sufficient One. Shame almost aborted the feeding of the 5000. They had just enough; but they were ashamed of it. Are you shamed that you cannot give what other people give? Are you embarrassed that others have worked this principle and you are now just gaining an understanding of it?

My advice in dealing with shame is that you become fully persuaded on the truth of what God's Word says about you and your potential. Choose to saturate yourself with Scriptural truth on giving and you will be persuaded that God sees your giving based on what you have done and not in comparison with what others are doing. Whatever you have to give, just give it! Don't ever discount your little bit! Remember, this is a principle as you work it; you will see more come into your life and then you will be able to give more. Just get started right where you are.

I am reminded of the story of one on my spiritual sons in the ministry who embraced this principle at a time in his life when he and his ministry were financially stretched. He was persuaded that this principle would be the key to his future success in life and ministry. He was the pastor of a small church in South Carolina and doing his best to make ends meet each month was a major feat. Even though it would take a sacrifice, he made the bold decision to embrace this principle to get God's help on his life and in his ministry.

Each month he would send a $5.00 money order in the mail. In comparison to what others sons in ministry were doing, He knew that what he had done was not significant. However, in comparison to what he had remaining, this was a significantly bountiful gift. Here we are years later and recently at this writing, I watched him give a public offering of $25,000! He would certainly testify that this giving principle really does work!

GRIEF

You would hardly think that the emotion of grief would be associated with the giving moment, but it can be when giving is seen as a major irrecoverable loss of something precious. This story of the rich ruler illustrates a giving appeal that was looked upon as a grievous moment.

When the rich young ruler came to Jesus, he was full of self-confidence! He came to Jesus seeking affirmation of his superior lifestyle. He confidently checked off a list of his spiritual credentials. However, when Jesus challenged his religious comfort zone, and placed a demand upon him, at this request, the rich young ruler retreated. Jesus challenged him by saying the following.

> "... One thing thou lackest: go thy way, sell whatsoever thou hast, and give to the poor, and thou shalt have treasure in heaven: and come, take up the cross, and follow me." (Mark 10:21)

> "And he was sad at that saying, and went away grieved: for he had great possessions." (Mark 10:22)

Why was he grieved? He saw giving as a loss and not a gain. But, a true giver understands that though the offering leaves their hands, it never leaves their lives. Whenever God asks you for something, it is not to take from you, but get something to you! Do you see that giving to someone is a waste, if has more than you? Do you question why you should have to give to the pastor because he or she gets a salary and doesn't really need it? Giving to your pastor is one sure way to gain! You should re-read the Scriptures I presented previously so that you can see your giving as an investment that must produce a return.

FRUSTRATION

Many believers are most frustrated with the giving and receiving aspect of the Gospel message because the receiving does not take place the same day. The delayed manifestation, the not knowing the source of the manifestation and the need of patience could make this process somewhat frustrating. An Old Testament story about the Prophet and his impatient spiritual son illustrates this point.

Gehazi was the servant to the Prophet Elisha. He stood by and watched this Prophet help so many people. On one occasion, a leprous foreigner named Naaman comes for healing. After initial resistance, Naaman complies with the Prophets' command and emerges from the water completely healed. In gratitude, Naaman offers the Prophet Elisha gold, silver, and clothes. But, the Prophet refuses. Gehazi becomes frustrated and devises a plan to steal the items through deceit. He was not seeing results from his giving and service and a sense of frustration arose. He would not wait for a righteous return on Kingdom investment. So, he sought to make a blessing for himself. He lied to Naaman about the arrival of unexpected guests who required provisions. Then, he sought to hide his deed from Elisha.

> "And when he came to the tower, he took them from their hand, and bestowed them in the house: and he let the men go, and they departed. But he went in, and stood before his master. And Elisha said unto him, Whence comest thou, Gehazi? And he said, Thy servant went no whither. And he said unto him, Went not mine heart with thee, when the man turned again from his chariot to meet thee? Is it a time to receive money, and to receive garments, and oliveyards, and vineyards, and sheep, and oxen, and menservants, and maidservants?"
> (2 Kings 5:34-36 KJV)

Because Gehazi acted on his frustrations, he lost his health, the trust of the man of God and the harvest on his faithful giving and service. Often people, who do not see immediate results, will become frustrated with this process how their giving-offerings work for them, especially when giving to the pastor. You must understand that even when the promised manifestation is delayed, it does not mean your faith is not working and that you have been denied. You must learn to stay in faith and continue to trust the process. Right on the other side of your frustration is the manifestation of the first-class lifestyle you desire, if you stick with it. The peace and contentment of being fully persuaded is the antidote for frustration.

> "And let us not be weary in well doing: for in due season we shall reap, if we faint not."
> (Galatians 6:9)

JEALOUSY

The jealousy emotion is probably the most common enemy emotion that people find themselves dealing with when it comes to this type of Kingdom giving. It is the unwarranted disdain one feels when observing the blessing or good fortune of another. In this case, the good fortunes of the pastor can be distasteful to those who are dealing with jealousy. One of the classical examples of this in Scripture is seen in the story of the woman with the alabaster box and giving this precious gift to Jesus. Judas observed it and the jealousy that he had kept hidden, surfaced in plain view to everyone!

Judas was the treasurer and he could not handle seeing Jesus get blessed. At the home of Lazarus, Jesus was sitting for a meal.

> *"Then took Mary a pound of ointment of spikenard, very costly, and anointed the feet of Jesus, and wiped his feet with her hair: and the house was filled with the odour of the ointment. Then saith one of his disciples, Judas Iscariot, Simon's son, which should betray him, Why was not this ointment sold for three hundred pence, and given to the poor?"*
> (John 12:3-5 KJV)

Now, Judas really did not care about the poor. He judged that Jesus was not worthy of such an extravagant gift! Judas' actions and heart condition had disqualified him for Kingdom increase and contentment, so he had to resort to stealing. So many people will stop giving because they see others walking in a level of prosperity they would like for themselves. Judas begrudged Jesus receiving this public display because his heart had become polluted by jealousy. This jealousy led him to betray Jesus to the Jewish leaders. Guard your heart against jealousy! Be careful not to count your pastor's financial wherewithal.

Jealousy is birthed from the misguided thinking that you are more worthy to receive, than the person you are jealous of. That's right, somehow the jealous person has illogically deduced that the person is unworthy to receive what they have. Further, the jealous person thinks that if another person has what they desire, their chance of acquiring the same or similar is lessened. The jealous of heart think others are undeserving and should not possess it. This emotion normally manifests as it did in Judas, through an intentional attempt to persuade others of the folly of their kind actions toward others.

Envy is often confused with jealousy; they are really kissing cousin emotions with one major difference. The major difference is that whereas jealousy desires to have what others have, envy does not. Envy just does not want to see others in a blessed state, though they don't desire to have it for themselves.

Don't be one of those persons who sits in service and calculates how much the pastor may be getting from the offering. Decide to intentionally rejoice over the blessings that come to your leader. Avoid those who are jealous and will attempt to corrupt your heart. Do not inspect if your pastor has new clothes, shoes, or cars. All of this will produce a sense of jealousy. Jealousy is rooted in a sense of God's inadequacy. God has enough that He can reward all those who support His servants! Your pastor's blessing does not diminish what God has for you.

You should want to sow into a pastor based on the principle and promises of God and not based on his or hers severe need. You are not a bad person because you have been tempted to be jealous of your pastor or his family. Temptation is not a sin, but yielding to the temptation is the sin. You must intentionally reject the thoughts of jealousy, take a positive action of prayer to confess it, followed by intentional actions of kindness.

I remember a jealousy attack on my heart years ago when I heard of a pastor I knew who had been given an aircraft. Wow! Someone actually gave it to him, free and clear, was what I was told. Immediately, my mind went there to jealous avenue and tried to park, but I would not let it. I thought, why did someone give a jet to him and not to me. I felt I was far more deserving and could make much better use of it. Well, immediately, I checked my heart, shouted aloud, "Devil you are a liar, my heart is off limits to that foolishness." I said, "Devil if you come at me with that thought again, I will call him up and buy him a tank of fuel as an act of kindness." Jealousy will corrupt your heart to the point where it will disqualify you from receiving from God.

GREED

Greed is a most dangerous enemy emotion because it has the potential of blinding you to your purpose, principles, and priorities. Most thieves are caught because of the greed factor; it is the consuming desire to have and possess by any means necessary. Greed is at the root of most Christians' disdain for giving because they are unwilling to part with what they have. Greed causes logic and reasoning to take the back seat, while it drives people into compromise and even criminal activity.

Joshua was leading the children of Israel against Jericho. God instructed Joshua that no spoils were to be kept from there, except the gold, silver, brass and iron, which was consecrated to the Lord. (Joshua 6:19) Everything else was marked for destruction. In their first significant victory, Achan could not understand how they couldn't enjoy some of the spoils. His greed caused Israel to lose a battle against Ai, a small city. Achan wanted it all. This is why a knowledgeable believer reasons that it is acceptable to not tithe! They have judged that God does not deserve anything! When exposed, he tried to offer an explanation.

> "And Achan answered Joshua, and said, Indeed I have sinned against the LORD God of Israel, and thus and thus have I done: When I saw among the spoils a goodly Babylonish garment, and two hundred shekels of silver, and a wedge of gold of fifty shekels weight, then I coveted them, and took them; and, behold, they are hid in the earth in the midst of my tent, and the silver under it."
> (Joshua 7:20-21 KJV)

Greed always backfires on itself. Achan thought he was gaining, but he ended up losing everything! Achan's lack of submission to his leader manifested in this rebellious act that was spawned by negative emotions.

Let me ask you some probing questions that will help reveal some possibly hidden negative emotions. Are you holding back from giving to your pastor because you are trying to amass more than he or she has? Are you trying to get to the top financially by hoarding? Do you think you are better than your pastor? Do you think that because you have more education, make more money, or carry a higher worldly title that you should not give? Are you above giving to your pastor?

When these malevolent emotions are overcome, you are ready to walk in a new level of supernatural abundance. One emotion that you should cultivate as you read this book is passion. I define passion as the diligent effort to accomplish a predetermined objective with the emotional strength of character to obey God, overcome problems, and possess the promises. Passion produces perseverance! You may not see results after the first gift to your pastor, but keep on giving. It must work. "Be not deceived; God is not mocked: for whatsoever a man soweth, that shall he also reap." (Galatians 6:7). I want you to gain a "fire in the belly" about giving money to your pastor, so that every time you see him or her, you will bring a seed.

At every point of giving, you have a choice to obey God, obey your feelings, or obey the devil. When you reject the opportunity to give to your pastor, you forfeit this proven avenue that God uses to get blessings to you!

SECTION TWO

The Conscious Choice - The Revelation

THE OBSERVATION OF HISTORY

In today's climate, the whole idea of turning aside to honor spiritual leadership in a tangible monetary way is at the height of controversy. To make matters worse, in an effort to stave off media scrutiny and persecution for living a blessed lifestyle, many high profile pastors openly celebrate that they do not take a salary from their churches. Unfortunately, there are those even in the Body of Christ who oppose the concept of honoring spiritual leadership because of a lack of Scriptural knowledge. Honoring spiritual leadership is just that, a spiritual matter; and those outside of the church of God will never be able to fully discern it. Somehow, we Believers have developed this need to have the world accept and understand our spiritual ways, which is diametrically opposed to what the Scripture teaches us to expect!

> *"But the natural, nonspiritual man does not accept or welcome or admit into his heart the gifts and teachings and revelations of the Spirit of God, for they are folly (meaningless nonsense) to him; and he is*

> incapable of knowing them [of progressively recognizing, understanding, and becoming better acquainted with them] because they are spiritually discerned and estimated and appreciated."
> (1 Corinthians 2:14 AMP)

In order to fully embrace this plan of God to tangibly honor spiritual leadership, you must accept that the ways of God are superior to man's ways and thoughts. Only when the Believer elevates the Word of God above traditions and prejudices, will there be an open mind to understand and accept the counsel of God on this matter.

> "For my thoughts are not your thoughts, neither are your ways my ways, saith the LORD. For as the heavens are higher than the earth, so are my ways higher than your ways, and my thoughts than your thoughts." (Isaiah 55:8-9 KJV)

I will present a Scriptural case for honoring your pastor and establish a righteous expectation of reward for those who will respect and live by this principle. My goal is to raise your consciousness to this Kingdom connection that is ordained by God for your benefit. Because you selected this book, I trust that you are willing to step into a new way of living. This is how the Apostle Paul approached this topic for the saints in the Corinthian church. They seemed to be confused on this honoring principle. Read this passage from the Apostle's letter to the church in Corinth.

> "This is my answer to those who question my authority. Don't we have the right to live in your homes and share your meals? Don't we have the right to bring a Christian wife with us as the other apostles and the Lord's brothers do, and as Peter does? Or is it only Barnabas and I who have to work to support ourselves? What soldier has to pay his own expenses? What farmer plants a vineyard and doesn't have the right to eat some of its fruit? What shepherd cares for a flock of sheep and isn't allowed to drink some of the milk? Am I expressing merely a human opinion, or does the law say the same thing? For the law of Moses says, 'You must not muzzle an ox to keep it from eating as it treads out the grain.' Was God thinking only about oxen when he said this? Wasn't he actually speaking to us? Yes, it was written for us, so that the one who plows and the one who threshes the grain might both expect a share of the harvest. Since we have planted spiritual seed among you, aren't we entitled to a harvest of physical food and drink? If you support others who preach to you, shouldn't we have an even greater right to be supported? But we have never used this right. We would rather put up with anything than be an obstacle to the Good News about Christ. Don't you realize that those who work in the temple get their meals from the offerings brought to the temple? And those who serve at the altar get a share of the sacrificial offerings.

> *In the same way, the Lord ordered that those who preach the Good News should be supported by those who benefit from it. Yet I have never used any of these rights. And I am not writing this to suggest that I want to start now. In fact, I would rather die than lose my right to boast about preaching without charge. Yet preaching the Good News is not something I can boast about. I am compelled by God to do it. How terrible for me if I didn't preach the Good News! If I were doing this on my own initiative, I would deserve payment. But I have no choice, for God has given me this sacred trust. What then is my pay? It is the opportunity to preach the Good News without charging anyone. That's why I never demand my rights when I preach the Good News."*
> (1Corinthians 9:3-18 NLT)

First let's take a spiritual look at the relationship between you and your spiritual leaders. You will discover that from God's point of view, this is a significant and dynamic relationship that is not to be taken lightly. The spiritual leader for the average Christian is their pastor, but this revelation is not at all limited to a pastor-member relationship. The Bible has much to say about the relationship between the pastor and member that I will take a moment to highlight.

> "And I will give you [spiritual] shepherds after My own heart [in the final time], who will feed you with knowledge and understanding and judgment."
> (Jeremiah 3:15 AMP)

> "Take heed therefore unto yourselves, and to all the flock, over the which the Holy Ghost hath made you overseers, to feed the church of God, which he hath purchased with his own blood. For I know this, that after my departing shall grievous wolves enter in among you, not sparing the flock. Also of your own selves shall men arise, speaking perverse things, to draw away disciples after them. Therefore watch, and remember, that by the space of three years I ceased not to warn every one night and day with tears." (Acts 20:28-31 KJV)

> "I WARN and counsel the elders among you (the pastors and spiritual guides of the church) as a fellow elder and as an eyewitness [called to testify] of the sufferings of Christ, as well as a sharer in the glory (the honor and splendor) that is to be revealed (disclosed, unfolded): Tend (nurture, guard, guide, and fold) the flock of God that is [your responsibility], not by coercion or constraint, but willingly; not dishonorably motivated by the advantages and profits [belonging to the office], but eagerly and cheerfully; Not domineering [as arrogant, dictatorial, and overbearing persons] over those in your charge, but being examples (patterns and models

> of Christian living) to the flock (the congregation). And [then] when the Chief Shepherd is revealed, you will win the conqueror's crown of glory." (1 Peter 5:1-4 AMP)

> "Obey your spiritual leaders and submit to them [continually recognizing their authority over you], for they are constantly keeping watch over your souls and guarding your spiritual welfare, as men who will have to render an account [of their trust]. [Do your part to] let them do this with gladness and not with sighing and groaning, for that would not be profitable to you [either]." (Hebrews 13:17 AMP)

These passages and others show that the pastor-member relationship is one of divine order and should not be taken lightly by either party. God uses the anointing on the spiritual leadership's life to benefit those to whom they are sent to minister. In making the quality decision to give proper honor to the pastoral gift under which you are set, it is refreshing to understanding the dynamics and purpose of the relationship.

It is indisputable from the previously mentioned Scriptures that God has ordained the office of the Pastor to serve in a divine spiritual role that is necessary for the Believer's growth, protection, and spiritual development. Scripture establishes that God uses pastors as agents to build faith in the congregation.

> *"How then shall they call on him in whom they have not believed? and how shall they believe in him of whom they have not heard? and how shall they hear without a preacher? And how shall they preach, except they be sent? as it is written, How beautiful are the feet of them that preach the Gospel of peace, and bring glad tidings of good things! But they have not all obeyed the Gospel. For Esaias saith, Lord, who hath believed our report? So then faith cometh by hearing, and hearing by the word of God." (Romans 10:14-17 KJV)*

Spiritual leadership, or pastor, is one of the key members in the fivefold ministry office to edify and bring the saints to a level of fruitfulness and maturity. The New Testament writers state that the pastor is placed to watch for the saints' souls and to serve as examples to the flock of the Gospel truth.

In a more practical sense, we depend on our pastors to be there for us during the challenging times of life. We rejoice that they are there to celebrate the birth of our children, dedicate them to God, and baptize them. Their prayers comfort us when we go through times of trouble and sickness. Their wisdom anchors us when we are going through seasons of relationship difficulty and hold us through stormy times. We hold to every word they speak to us during the times of bereavement when a loved one passes away. Their value to us is really priceless and should never be taken for granted.

Scripture shows how God has used spiritual leaders to rescue people from times of devastation and even death. The last thing we should do is to undermine the significance and importance of our spiritual leaders because it would contradict Scripture to do so. The Old Testament is filled with stories where God used the prophets to bring deliverance, relief, and miracles to his covenant people.

THE DEBT MIRACLE STORY

The amazing story in 2 Kings 4 of a widow was left in overwhelming debt by her late husband. The creditors were about to take her sons into debt servitude because she was unable to satisfy the debt. The widow goes to the prophet, her spiritual leader, for wisdom, ministry, and a plan of action. The instructions that he gave her turned her situation around, saved her family, and brought her out of debt.

THE JEHOSHAPHAT STORY

In 2 Chronicles 20, it was the counsel from the Prophet Jahaziel, spiritual leader to Jehoshaphat, that ushered in the victory for Jehoshaphat when he was outnumbered by his enemies. The tide of the battle turned upon the prophetic words by the Prophet, thus proving the importance of spiritual leadership's role in the victory. This often quoted passage of 2 Chronicles 20:20 originates from this event.

> *"And they rose early in the morning, and went forth into the wilderness of Tekoa: and as they went*

> forth, Jehoshaphat stood and said, Hear me, O Judah, and ye inhabitants of Jerusalem; Believe in the LORD your God, so shall ye be established; believe his prophets, so shall ye prosper."
> (2 Chronicles 20:20 KJV)

THE WIDOW OF ZAREPHATH'S STORY

The importance of the prophet Elijah is clearly seen in the story of the widow of Zarephath in 1 Kings 17. The scene is quite intense, there was a famine in the land; the Prophet was sent to the widow while she is in a desperate situation. She and her son were about to die of starvation with only one meal left. The Prophet ministers faith to her and she obeys his instructions. After her obedience to the affirming words of the Prophet, she and her household received a miracle. They received enough provisions to sustain them during the famine.

It is more than safe to conclude that in the all-wise counsel of God, He has instituted the relationship between spiritual leader and people for their mutual benefit. The benefit is far greater than the counsel, wisdom, and comforting ministry of the leader to the follower. There is a supernatural dimension to this connection that many have yet to realize. The purpose of this book is to unveil this Scriptural revelation, so that you and others can begin to benefit.

THE OBLIGATION TO HONOR

Giving honor to spiritual leadership who blesses us, is not a suggestion; it is a mandate. Both the Old and New Testament have references and examples of honor being given to spiritual leadership. Honor is a dynamic term used in Scripture to mean giving fitting and due RESPECT, fitting and due RECOGNITION, but also, giving fitting and due RESOURCES to others. The Scripture instructs Believers to honor God, to honor parents, to honor the elders, to honor rulers, and to honor spiritual leaders. There is an indisputable blessing that rebounds upon those who honor their spiritual leaders.

THE MANDATE TO HONOR

Look at these Scriptural instructions given to the New Testament Believers about honoring those in leadership. These passages will serve to confirm that we should never take for granted those in spiritual leadership and they clearly show that they should receive special honor. Read these passages because they accurately reflect the mandate to give respect, recognition, and resources as a proper way to demonstrate honor.

> "And now, friends, we ask you to honor those leaders who work so hard for you, who have been given the responsibility of urging and guiding you along in your obedience. Overwhelm them with appreciation and love! Get along among yourselves, each of you doing your part."
> (1 Thessalonians 5:12-13 MSG)

> "Let the elders who perform the duties of their office well be considered doubly worthy of honor [and of

adequate financial support], especially those who labor faithfully in preaching and teaching. For the Scripture says, You shall not muzzle an ox when it is treading out the grain, and again, The laborer is worthy of his hire." (1 Timothy 5:17-18 AMP)

"Let him who receives instruction in the Word [of God] share all good things with his teacher [contributing to his support]." (Galatians 6:6 AMP)

"As you well know, when I first brought the Gospel to you and then went on my way, leaving Macedonia, only you Philippians became my partners in giving and receiving. No other church did this. Even when I was over in Thessalonica you sent help twice. But though I appreciate your gifts, what makes me happiest is the well-earned reward you will have because of your kindness." (Philippians 4:15-17 LBT)

"Obey your spiritual leaders and submit to them [continually recognizing their authority over you], for they are constantly keeping watch over your souls and guarding your spiritual welfare, as men who will have to render an account [of their trust]. [Do your part to] let them do this with gladness and not with sighing and groaning, for that would not be profitable to you [either]." (Hebrews 13:7 AMP)

Honoring spiritual leadership is expressed in a multifaceted manner in Scripture. For clarity's sake, let's examine a few passages that show how spiritual leaders, prophets, priests, and pastors were honored with resources. Most people don't have much of a problem with giving recognition to leadership for job well done or the giving of respect for job well done, but when it comes to tangible resources, that is where most people have a disconnect. As I outlined in the previous section, there is a disdain in giving material resources to spiritual leaders. Most secular people are comfortable with spiritual leaders living a blessed life, so long as they do not derive their lifestyle from the salary they receive from the ministry.

Unfortunately, people who hold this view have no idea of the plan of God that is prescribed in the Bible. God has ordained that those who minister the Gospel should be taken care of by those they lead. It amazes me that society is comfortable with the basketball player who is supported from the sport that he plays, even with ticket prices continuing to rise. No one expects an attorney to handle her client base without compensation from those whom she serves. Even television celebrities are compensated by and based upon their fan base. Many CEO's of large non-profit corporations are remunerated very nicely and their executive package would surpass what most mega church pastors receive from the funds that come through the organization. So then, why is there a double standard as it relates to pastors and comparable compensation? Could it be that there is a demonic scheme in place to dishonor the most vital relationship in the Believer's life? Let's examine the Word of God to determine if He ordains, instructs, and validates His appointed spiritual leaders receiving from the people to whom they minister.

ABRAHAM HONORS THE PRIEST BY GIVING HIM A TITHE

> "Melchizedek king of Salem [later called Jerusalem] brought out bread and wine [for their nourishment]; he was the priest of God Most High, And he blessed him and said, Blessed (favored with blessings, made blissful, joyful) be Abram by God Most High, Possessor and Maker of heaven and earth, And blessed, praised, and glorified be God Most High, Who has given your foes into your hand! And [Abram] gave him a tenth of all [he had taken]."
> (Genesis 14:18-20 AMP)

As far back as Abram, we can see this principle at work. After a great victory, he seeks out the priest of his day to give an offering, so that he would be partaker of divine blessings. We will see this modeled throughout the pages of Biblical history. There are many confirming Scriptural witnesses that I will present. So, read on.

THE WIDOW HONORS THE PROPHETS BY GIVING HIM HER LAST

> "So he arose and went to Zarephath. And when he came to the gate of the city, behold, the widow woman was there gathering of sticks: and he called to her, and said, Fetch me, I pray thee, a little water

> in a vessel, that I may drink. And as she was going to fetch it, he called to her, and said, Bring me, I pray thee, a morsel of bread in thine hand. And she said, As the LORD thy God liveth, I have not a cake, but an handful of meal in a barrel, and a little oil in a cruse: and, behold, I am gathering two sticks, that I may go in and dress it for me and my son, that we may eat it, and die. And Elijah said unto her, Fear not; go and do as thou hast said: but make me thereof a little cake first, and bring it unto me, and after make for thee and for thy son. For thus saith the LORD God of Israel, The barrel of meal shall not waste, neither shall the cruse of oil fail, until the day that the LORD sendeth rain upon the earth. And she went and did according to the saying of Elijah: and she, and he, and her house, did eat many days. And the barrel of meal wasted not, neither did the cruse of oil fail, according to the word of the LORD, which he spake by Elijah."
>
> (1Kings 17:10-16 KJV)

This is a popular preaching text; unfortunately, the truth that it conveys, escapes most people. God assigned the widow to provide for the Prophet of God. It is always the order of God that the people of God care for God's servants who minister to them. When Elijah arrived, he was fully aware of the miraculous potential of this connection, if the woman would do her part. This simple truth is that our obedience authorizes God to get involved. In today's media climate, the prophet would have been highly criticized as the "Preacher Who Took The Poor Widow's Last." Knowing that her obedience to this principle was the key to her supernatural sustenance, he stood his ground and made the bold request that she obey God. His ministry to her helped her overcome her fears and reservations so that she could obey God. What an awesome model to the contemporary church; giving this gift caused the amazing breakthrough for her and her family that day. Since God is not a respecter of persons, he is obligated to move in our situations on the basis of our sacrificial offering in support of our spiritual leaders. There are even more examples.

SAUL HONORS THE PROPHET BY GIVING HIM MONEY

> *"And he said unto him, Behold now, there is in this city a man of God, and he is an honourable man; all that he saith cometh surely to pass: now let us go thither; peradventure he can shew us our way that we should go. Then said Saul to his servant, But, behold, if we go, what shall we bring the man? for the bread is spent in our vessels, and there is not a present to bring to the man of God: what have we? And the servant answered Saul again, and said, Behold, I have here at hand the fourth part of a shekel of silver: that will I give to the man of God, to tell us our way. (Beforetime in Israel, when a man went to enquire of God, thus he spake, Come, and let us go to the seer: for he that is now called a Prophet was beforetime called a Seer.) Then said Saul to his servant, Well said; come, let us go. So*

> they went unto the city where the man of God was."
> (1 Samuel 9:6-10 KJV)

This story, which is secreted away in the Old Testament, shows the respect for the prophet, the spiritual leaders in those days. They would not solicit his wisdom without having something to give. The precedent was established and respected by those who did not have the Scriptural proof we have today. Moreover, they were not graced with the Holy Spirit as their resident guide; yet, they knew to provide a financial gift to the prophet. You are about to read an account where God incorporated in the Law of Moses a provision, which clearly states that the people were to give financial substance to the priests.

IN THE LAW, GOD INSTRUCTS THE PEOPLE TO GIVE REGULARLY TO THE PRIESTS

> "It's the Levites and only the Levites who are to work in the Tent of Meeting and they are responsible for anything that goes wrong. This is the regular rule for all time. They get no inheritance among the People of Israel; instead I turn over to them the tithes that the People of Israel present as an offering to God. That's why I give the ruling: They are to receive no land-inheritance among the People of Israel. God spoke to Moses: 'Speak to the Levites. Tell them, When you get the tithe from the People of Israel, the inheritance that I have assigned to you, you must tithe that tithe and present it as an offering to God. Your offerings will be treated

> the same as other people's gifts of grain from the threshing floor or wine from the wine vat. This is your procedure for making offerings to God from all the tithes you get from the People of Israel: give God's portion from these tithes to Aaron the priest. Make sure that God's portion is the best and holiest of everything you get.' " (Numbers 18:23-29 KJV)

In the plan of God for Israel, His emancipated people were taught that they would observe worship in specific ways. In the Law of Moses, God forthrightly addresses the compensation of spiritual leadership. The Law of God, as recorded by Moses, reflects the intent of God's heart and the intent must be respected in all dispensations. There were twelve tribes of Israel, which were birthed from the twelve sons of Jacob (Israel). All of these tribes, except the Levitical tribe, were given territory in the Promised Land, so that they would blossom, grow, and prosper. The Levitical Tribe was the priestly tribe, which held the unique responsibility of handling the worship sacrifices, rituals, and the sanctuary. God specifically states that their prosperity and sustenance was to be derived directly from what the people gave to them. Their inheritance was not in lands and property, but their faithfulness of service would be cared for, through the tithes and offerings of all the people of Israel. This further establishes the order of God that spiritual leadership receives support from the congregation who he serves.

THE FIRST FRUITS OFFERING WAS GIVEN TO THE PROPHETS

> *"And the first of all the firstfruits of all things, and every oblation of all, of every sort of your oblations, shall be the priest's: ye shall also give unto the priest the first of your dough, that he may cause the blessing to rest in thine house."* (Ezekiel 44:30 KJV)

> *"[At another time] a man from Baal-shalisha came and brought the man of God bread of the firstfruits, twenty loaves of barley, and fresh ears of grain [in the husk] in his sack. And Elisha said, Give to the men that they may eat. His servant said, How am I to set [only] this before a hundred [hungry] men? He said, Give to the men that they may eat. For thus says the Lord: They shall be fed and have some left. So he set it before them, and they ate and left some, as the Lord had said."*
> (2 Kings 4:42-44 AMP)

I am well aware of the present controversy concerning the First-fruit offerings. This book neither addresses the controversy nor how it was to be gathered. What is crystal clear in the Scripture is that under the Law of Moses the First-fruit offerings were to be brought to the priest. The second passage shows that the Prophet Elisha received the First-fruit offering. Again, contrary to popular worldly opinion, the Scripture establishes that it is the order of God to bring offerings to ordained spiritual leadership. This next story is often quoted in church, but the truth of this couple's generosity to the prophet is over looked.

THE SHUNNAMITE (SHUNEM) WOMAN GIVES THE PROPHET A GIFT

> "One day Elisha passed through Shunem. A leading lady of the town talked him into stopping for a meal. And then it became his custom: Whenever he passed through, he stopped by for a meal. 'I'm certain,' said the woman to her husband, 'that this man who stops by with us all the time is a holy man of God. Why don't we add on a small room upstairs and furnish it with a bed and desk, chair and lamp, so that when he comes by he can stay with us?' And so it happened that the next time Elisha came by he went to the room and lay down for a nap." (2 Kings 4:8-11 MSG)

After reading this account of a husband and wife jointly agreeing to do something special to honor the Prophet Elisha, we see that honoring spiritual leadership should be a family affair. This couple constructed a room in their house, especially for the prophet. They properly furnished it so that it would provide rest and relaxation for the man of God as he traveled. This story affirms that all material blessings given to spiritual leadership are not always monetary. It is obvious that the Prophet appreciated this gift because the Scripture notes that every time he passed that way, he took advantage of the prophet's quarters they provided.

For those who think that giving tangible gifts to God's servants lessens their commitment to ministry will find the next Scripture compelling. This is the story of the partners of Jesus and how they freely offered their resources. Read this passage and be enlightened.

> ### THE WOMEN GIVE MONEY (RESOURCES) TO JESUS
>
> *"And also some women who had been cured of evil spirits and diseases: Mary, called Magdalene, from whom seven demons had been expelled; And Joanna, the wife of Chuza, Herod's household manager; and Susanna; and many others, who ministered to and provided for Him and them out of their property and personal belongings."*
> (Luke 8:2-3 MSG)

If this story does not settle the issue for you, then no other Scripture will resolve this matter. Here, we have the Lord Jesus Himself receiving personal gifts from those who followed Him. We will see later how Jesus taught that giving a cup of water to spiritual leaders would result in a reciprocal blessing. It is an undeniable truth that Jesus afforded his followers an opportunity to give tangible gifts to support His team and Him. The mistaken notion that Jesus was financially destitute is unthinkable! How can you reconcile a poor preacher, with a poor ministry, handling the daily physical needs a staff of at least 12 men (or up to 70 men), during a year of His most impactful ministry?

This was not the only occasion when Jesus accepted a tangible gift of appreciation from a follower. As you will see, one of His followers publicly gave Him a significant gift, which caused a controversy, and He addressed it.

THE WOMAN HONORS JESUS WITH EXPENSIVE ANOINTING PERFUME

> *"And being in Bethany in the house of Simon the leper, as he sat at meat, there came a woman having an alabaster box of ointment of spikenard very precious; and she brake the box, and poured it on his head. And there were some that had indignation within themselves, and said, Why was this waste of the ointment made? For it might have been sold for more than three hundred pence, and have been given to the poor. And they murmured against her. And Jesus said, Let her alone; why trouble ye her? she hath wrought a good work on me. For ye have the poor with you always, and whensoever ye will ye may do them good: but me ye have not always. She hath done what she could: she is come aforehand to anoint my body to the burying. Verily I say unto you, Wheresoever this Gospel shall be preached throughout the whole world, this also that she hath done shall be spoken of for a memorial of her."* (Mark 14:3-9 KJV)

Jesus ostensibly was in support of this gift, even though by the account of those present, it was extremely expensive. Jesus addressed those who assessed this gift as a waste with an open rebuke. Now we are not saying that gifts given today to your spiritual leaders carries the same level of significance as this gift to Jesus, but we are establishing that an expensive gift being given to a spiritual leader is not inappropriate. On another occasion, one of Jesus' Disciples endeavored to gather money to pay the temple tax for Jesus and ends up with enough money to pay his temple tax too. This story shows a spiritual leader receiving money from one of his followers to pay his temple tax.

PETER GIVES MONEY HE ACQUIRED TO PAY JESUS' TEMPLE TAXES

> "When they arrived in Capernaum, the collectors of the half shekel [the temple tax] went up to Peter and said, Does not your Teacher pay the half shekel? He answered, Yes. And when he came home, Jesus spoke to him [about it] first, saying, What do you think, Simon? From whom do earthly rulers collect duties or tribute—from their own sons or from others not of their own family? And when Peter said, From other people not of their own family, Jesus said to him, Then the sons are exempt. However, in order not to give offense and cause them to stumble [that is, to cause them to judge unfavorably and unjustly] go down to the sea and throw in a hook. Take the first fish that comes up, and when you open its mouth you will find there a shekel. Take it and give it to them to pay the temple tax for Me and for yourself."
> (Matthew 17:24-27 KJV)

In each example, it is clear to see that Scripture validates honoring spiritual leadership with financial gifts. The final case study will be the story of the Apostle Paul applauding the Philippians for their consistent giving to support him as their spiritual leader.

THE PHILIPPIANS GIVE MONEY TO THE APOSTLE PAUL

> *"As you well know, when I first brought the Gospel to you and then went on my way, leaving Macedonia, only you Philippians became my partners in giving and receiving. No other church did this. Even when I was over in Thessalonica you sent help twice. But though I appreciate your gifts, what makes me happiest is the well-earned reward you will have because of your kindness."*
> (Philippians 4:15-17 LBT)

When the Apostle Paul wanted to use a church as a model for other churches concerning giving, he would refer to the Philippian Church in the Macedonia region. (2 Corinthians 8:1-7) It is clear that this church regularly gave to him for his personal support when no other church did. Paul encourages them to do so not solely for the benefit he receives from the gifts, but for the blessing that is promised to rebound back into their lives.

It is undeniable by both precept and example that it is the order of God for spiritual leaders to receive material and financial support from God's covenant people. To believe anything other than this would require that you, as a Christian, have another authority outside of the Word of God and that would be heresy. The motivation that God has attached to this giving has been the reciprocal blessing that is promised to those who will honor their spiritual leadership.

Whenever there is a mandate of supreme importance, that mandate is normally supported with a promised blessing. Think about it, we are all encouraged by the attainment of a reward or blessing. The support and the sustaining of ordained spiritual leadership is of such importance to God that He attaches a reciprocal blessing as motivation to obey. The final part of this section will address the promised harvest given to those who will give to spiritual leadership.

THE OBLIGATED HARVEST FOR THOSE WHO HONOR

Before we get into the specifics of the blessings bestowed on those who will honor their pastors and spiritual leaders, let's look at the power of honoring as it is addressed in Scripture. The principle of honor is much more dynamic as seen in this passage from the Old Testament where God establishes that those who will honor Him will be honored themselves.

> *"... But now the Lord says, Be it far from Me. For those who honor Me I will honor, and those who despise Me shall be lightly esteemed."*
> *(1 Samuel 2:30b KJV)*

Jesus, on the other hand, makes the statement during His ministry that people who honor those whom the Father sends, it is equal to honoring the Father Himself. The word 'received' in the text below is equal to the word 'honor' and thus, it makes a very powerful analogy.

> *"I assure you, most solemnly I tell you, he who receives and welcomes and takes into his heart any messenger of Mine receives Me [in just that way]; and he who receives and welcomes and takes Me into his heart receives Him Who sent Me [in that same way]. Then said Jesus to them again, Peace be unto you: as my Father hath sent me, even so send I you." (John 13:20-21 AMP)*

We know that the Father sent Jesus. Those who honor those that Jesus sends (spiritual leaders) are honoring Jesus himself. When we honor Jesus, it is also an honor to the Father. When the Father is honored, the Scripture says that He commits to honor those who honor Him! This is a powerful statement of the true dynamics of honor. Honoring others that God sends obligates Him to bless and honor them in return.

What motivated me years ago when I began to sow into my Pastor, were the many references to rewards and blessings that would be endowed on those who would support spiritual leadership. In just about every case listed previously, there is an accompanying promise of a blessing or the manifestation of a blessing. I have shared my personal testimony of how giving to my man of God has accelerated my success, but now walk with me through the pages of the Bible to see this in an undeniable way.

In the case of Abram who gave to the Priest Melchizedek, a blessing was spoken over his life and in the next chapter, we see Abram receiving a revelation on his destiny. In a subsequent chapter, Abram received many tangible blessings from the Lord. We have a legitimate right to connect the blessed vision that followed because the chapter begins, "After these things".

In the case of the Widow who gave her last for the support of the Prophet, a supernatural blessing manifested just as the Prophet declared. Her offering of obedience set into motion miracle provisions for her and her household, which kept her through the famine. Again, a gift to the man of God is rewarded by supernatural increase.

> "And she went and did according to the saying of Elijah: and she, and he, and her house, did eat many days. And the barrel of meal wasted not, neither did the cruse of oil fail, according to the word of the LORD, which he spake by Elijah."
> (1 Kings 17:15-16 KJV)

In the case of Saul who would become the King of Israel, he honors the Prophet with a respectable offering, and, in return, he gets a prophetic word that helps him locate his father's livestock. In addition, the man of God spoke direction into his life. This word that he received helped position him to receive the anointing to be the King of Israel.

Next, when the instructions for giving the First fruit offering were given, God incorporated in this offering the promise of a blessing be pronounced over the giver's heart!

> *"And the first of all the firstfruits of all things, and every oblation of all, of every sort of your oblations, shall be the priest's: ye shall also give unto the priest the first of your dough, that he may cause the blessing to rest in thine house." (Ezekiel 44:30 KJV)*

When we examine the story of the woman and her husband who provided lodging for the prophet as he passed by, the end of this episode validates again that giving personal resources to spiritual leadership will rebound blessings back into the life of the giver. In this case, the couple that had been barren for a long time was blessed with a child for their acts of kindness to this spiritual leadership.

> *"One day he came and turned into the chamber and lay there. And he said to Gehazi his servant, Call this Shunammite. When he had called her, she stood before him. And he said to Gehazi, Say now to her, You have been most painstakingly and reverently concerned for us; what is to be done for you? Would you like to be spoken for to the king or to the commander of the army? She answered, I dwell among my own people [they are sufficient]. Later Elisha said, What then is to be done for her? Gehazi answered, She has no child and her husband is old. He said, Call her. [Gehazi] called her, and she stood in the doorway. Elisha said, At this season when the time comes round, you shall embrace a son. She said, No, my lord, you man of God, do not lie to your handmaid. But the*

> woman conceived and bore a son at that season the following year, as Elisha had said to her."
> (2 Kings 4:11-17 AMP)

Reading this passage from 2 Kings further supports that God chooses to bless those who will honor spiritual leadership that He sends into their lives. The next story that helps support this point is the story of Jesus and Peter recorded it in Matthew 17. Jesus has an unpaid temple tax liability. Peter goes to work at the direction of Jesus to get money to pay the debt for Jesus and receives enough for his personal temple tax debt as well. As Peter worked to help Jesus, his spiritual leader, his efforts paid off in a tangible blessing of increase for himself.

> "However, in order not to give offense and cause them to stumble [that is, to cause them to judge unfavorably and unjustly] go down to the sea and throw in a hook. Take the first fish that comes up, and when you open its mouth you will find there a shekel. Take it and give it to them to pay the temple tax for Me and for yourself." (Matthew 17:27 KJV)

The final evidential story I will present in this section is the story of the blessing that the Apostle Paul pronounced on the church at Philippi, as a result of their faithfulness to personally support him. We hear this Scripture commonly quoted by those in the body of Christ, but is a promise that is restricted to those who qualify by their tangible financial support of their spiritual leadership. The 19th verse is what is most quoted, but read the verses that precede it.

> "For even in Thessalonica ye sent once and again unto my necessity. Not because I desire a gift: but I desire fruit that may abound to your account. But I have all, and abound: I am full, having received of Epaphroditus the things which were sent from you, an odour of a sweet smell, a sacrifice acceptable, wellpleasing to God. But my God shall supply all your need according to his riches in glory by Christ Jesus. Now unto God and our Father be glory for ever and ever. Amen." (Philippians 4:16-20 KJV)

Now read this same passage from the Living Bible, and you must agree that it does appear that even though Paul has more than he needs at that present moment he allows them to continue to give. Paul stresses that it is not so much that he needs, but the emphasis is that their giving causes fruit to abound to their account, for which God will bless them. So many blessed Pastors are robbing the people of this promised blessing; they attempted to escape the critics by refusing to accept a salary from their church.

> "Even when I was over in Thessalonica you sent help twice. But though I appreciate your gifts, what makes me happiest is the well-earned reward you will have because of your kindness. At the moment I have all I need--more than I need! I am generously

> supplied with the gifts you sent me when Epaphroditus came. They are a sweet-smelling sacrifice that pleases God well. And it is he who will supply all your needs from his riches in glory because of what Christ Jesus has done for us. Now unto God our Father be glory forever and ever. Amen."
>
> (Philippians 4:16-20 LB)

The passage elucidates that this type of giving is well pleasing to God. This should answer all the critics who would want to say that God is not pleased with people giving to their spiritual leaders. This is a consistent teaching of the Scripture; those who will accept the truth of the Bible must submit their personal feelings to this truth. During the teaching of Jesus, he boldly declares, as previously mentioned, that not so much as a cup of water given to leadership will go unnoticed and unrewarded by the Father.

> "He who receives and welcomes and accepts you receives and welcomes and accepts Me, and he who receives and welcomes and accepts Me receives and welcomes and accepts Him Who sent Me. He who receives and welcomes and accepts a prophet because he is a prophet shall receive a prophet's reward, and he who receives and welcomes and accepts a righteous man because he is a righteous man shall receive a righteous man's reward. And whoever gives to one of these little ones [in rank or influence] even a cup of cold water because he is My disciple, surely

> *I declare to you, he shall not lose his reward."*
> *(Matthew 10:40-42 AMP)*

When I look back over my life and how I faithfully served every spiritual leader under whom I was set, it is refreshing to see the faithfulness of God. Today, I know that I am blessed because I was faithful and much of what I am experiencing now is the result of the service, the submission and the substance that I have given to the men of God I have served. Despite the criticism, I can say that with the persecution and the sacrifice of time, it was worth it all for the return on the investment that I am now receiving.

I remember doing so much for my pastors and mentors for which I never was paid. I was serving out of a pure heart and genuine love for them, not knowing that God was taking notice. I drove them around like a chauffeur. I had personally funded their recording ministry (in the old 8 track days). Each year, I assembled their children's toys without remuneration! I made myself available to their beckoning call. I endured being called their "flunky," their "boy," and other names not appropriate to print in this book. I am blessed today with more than enough help because I sowed into the lives of my spiritual leaders. I will let the Scripture text from the book of Galatians close this section.

> *"Don't be misled: No one makes a fool of God. What a person plants, he will harvest. The person*

who plants selfishness, ignoring the needs of others—ignoring God!— harvests a crop of weeds. All he'll have to show for his life is weeds! But the one who plants in response to God, letting God's Spirit do the growth work in him, harvests a crop of real life, eternal life. So let's not allow ourselves to get fatigued doing good. At the right time we will harvest a good crop if we don't give up, or quit."
(Galatians 6:7-9 MSG)

: SECTION THREE

The Criteria Component - The Recognition

Now that you have received the revelation of the importance of giving honor to your spiritual leadership through tangible gifts, it is vital for us to spend some time looking at the qualifications for those who serve as spiritual leadership. This section is not designed to give you ammunition to judge your pastor. However, it is an affirmation of what the Biblical role of your pastor is supposed to be, so that you can more fully appreciate the gift that God has sent into your life. There is so much confusion about the role and responsibility of your spiritual leadership. Now, I want to attempt to clarify that from a Scriptural perspective.

THE REQUIREMENTS GIVEN FOR THE HONOREE

Here is what you should look for in your man and woman of God. Jeremiah 3:15 shows us that shepherds are a gift from God.

> *"And I will give you shepherds according to My heart, who will feed you with knowledge and understanding."*
> *(Jeremiah 3:15)*

The key pre-qualifier is that the person whom we honor has a track record of feeding us with the Word of God. The pastor does not need to be our friend. He or she does not need to socialize with us. He or she may not visit us in the hospital or in our homes. This aspect of ministry may be delegated to qualified staff. The primary role of the shepherd is to care for the flock by feeding them well from the Word of God, so that they mature into the people God created them to be.

> "And He Himself gave some to be apostles, some prophets, some evangelists, and some pastors and teachers, for the equipping of the saints for the work of ministry, for the edifying of the body of Christ, till we all come to the unity of the faith and of the knowledge of the Son of God, to a perfect man, to the measure of the stature of the fullness of Christ; we should no longer be children, tossed to and fro and carried about with every wind of doctrine, by the trickery of men, in the cunning craftiness of deceitful plotting." (Ephesians 4:11-14)

Here is a very important correction. Your pastor's responsibility is to teach you! It is your responsibility to learn! There is a difference. So many people say, "I'm not growing" and they immediately blame their pastor. There are two dimensions to growth: teaching and learning. When the truth of God's Word is presented to you weekly, it will not do you good if you don't receive it and put it into action (that's the learning part). No one controls learning but you! Once you are given a hearty Biblical diet, you have to do your part to internalize the lessons you have learned. Your pastor cannot control your level of acceptance and application.

So let me ask you: Do you respect your pastor as someone sent from God for your growth and development? Do you allow your pastor's teachings to impact your life by listening to their messages on a daily basis?

Your pastor watches for your soul. In other words, the servant of God placed in your life watches out for you spiritually. This is why the word 'Shepherd' is used to describe this role. A shepherd cares for the flock. He or she is concerned about your well-being—spiritually and naturally. When you stay connected to your Pastor and the vision of the church in which you are set, then you will hear a word that speaks directly to your situation and will hold the key to your protection and prosperity.

> *"Obey them that have the rule over you, and submit yourselves: for they watch for your souls, as they that must give account, that they may do it with joy, and not with grief: for that is unprofitable for you."*
> *(Hebrews 13:17)*

Notice here that God places a burden of responsibility upon those who would care for His people. Pastors will have to give an account for the actions they undertake. This is why you should never set yourself in a position to judge your pastor. This is not your role. God will judge His servants. Your responsibility is to follow the Biblical principles that you are taught and trust God to handle the rest.

Over the years, I have heard many people question, "What is my purpose?" Year after year, they sit in a church questioning their purpose. The interesting thing is that the vision of your church establishes your purpose. When you grasp that God sets you in a church as it pleases Him, you will be more discerning about the decisions you make to partner with a ministry and, if it is time to leave, you will do it with honor and respect.

> *"But now hath God set the members every one of them in the body, as it hath pleased him."*
> *(1 Corinthians 12:18)*

When you are a part of a ministry, all you need to do is passionately follow that vision and God's unique purpose for your life will emerge.

> *"And a vision appeared to Paul in the night; There stood a man of Macedonia, and prayed him, saying, Come over into Macedonia, and help us. And after he had seen the vision, immediately we endeavoured to go into Macedonia, assuredly gathering that the Lord had called us for to preach the Gospel unto them." (Acts 15:9-10)*

Those who were with Paul heard him recount what God

showed him in a vision. They never saw the vision and had no evidence that what Paul saw was authentic. However, they understood the importance of being aligned with God's vision. So, because Paul had seen the vision, those with him adopted that vision as their own and they went with Paul to Macedonia. Whatever God has called your pastor to do, he has called you to do as well!

One of the main reasons why they could trust Paul's vision was because they trusted him. He was a man of honor. He had a genuine conversion experience and Paul's love for God was evident with all who encountered him. Your pastor is an honorable person. Earlier, we looked at the woman from Shunem who testified about Elisha.

> "And she said to her husband, 'Look now, I know that this is a holy man of God, who passes by us regularly.' " (1 Kings 4:9)

This should be the testimony that you have of your man or woman of God. Honor is always fitting for those who walk before us as holy.

In the Old Testament, those appraised as worthy of honor had impeccable character and spiritual integrity. Let's look at an example below.

> "Now the donkeys of Kish, Saul's father, were lost. And Kish said to his son Saul, 'Please, take one of

> the servants with you, and arise, go and look for the donkeys.' So he passed through the mountains of Ephraim and through the land of Shalisha, but they did not find them. Then they passed through the land of Shaalim, and they were not there. Then he passed through the land of the Benjamites, but they did not find them. When they had come to the land of Zuph, Saul said to his servant who was with him, 'Come, let us return, lest my father cease caring about the donkeys and become worried about us.' And he said to him, 'Look now, there is in this city a man of God, and he is an honorable man; all that he says surely comes to pass. So let us go there; perhaps he can show us the way that we should go.' Then Saul said to his servant, 'But look, if we go, what shall we bring the man? For the bread in our vessels is all gone, and there is no present to bring to the man of God. What do we have?' And the servant answered Saul again and said, 'Look, I have here at hand one fourth of a shekel of silver. I will give that to the man of God, to tell us our way.' " (1 Samuel 9:3-8)

When people experienced challenging predicaments, they sought out wisdom and counsel from a Prophet of God. Back then, just like today, there were true prophets and false prophets. The distinguishing mark was if what they said came to pass. Samuel was known as a true Prophet and worthy of honor. He was respected as a Man of God from whom people could gain wisdom. You will also notice that they would never approach the man of God without bringing a gift to honor him. Samuel, like your pastor, should be respected for righteousness and integrity. Your pastor should be a demonstration of sound Biblical-based living. In essence, he or she should be an example. The New Testament affirms this in principle when referencing church leadership.

> "Let the elders who perform the duties of their office well be considered doubly worthy of honor [and of adequate financial support], especially those who labor faithfully in preaching and teaching. For the Scripture says, You shall not muzzle an ox when it is treading out the grain, and again, The laborer is worthy of his hire." (1 Timothy 5:17-18 AMP)

Your pastor is worthy of adequate financial support because he or she works faithfully in preaching and teaching. Those who honor God with diligent service are worthy to receive honor from those he or she serves. The one who has been assigned to teach you is worthy of your financial support.

> "Let him who receives instruction in the Word [of God] share all good things with his teacher [contributing to his support]." (Galatians 6:6 AMP)

In the same way that the priests in the Old Testament were supported by the offerings of the worshippers, so the New Testament Believer is commanded to financially support their pastors through consistent, regular offerings.

In summary, your pastor is worthy of financial support because they love you, teach you the Word of God and live as an example before you. If you have a pastor like this, then from a Biblical perspective, he or she is well qualified to receive your financial investment.

THE RESISTANCE TO GIVING THE HONOR

Unfortunately, just because a principle is clearly seen in the Bible, it is not universally accepted. You will be persecuted for obeying God's Word, especially in the area of your finances. Do you ever find it amazing that your friends will encourage you to use credit that you cannot pay to purchase items that you do not need? These same friends will receive your generosity in paying for meals, buying them gifts, and living a lifestyle beyond your means. They will even encourage going to expensive events of entertainment or concerts. Yet, when you mention that you are a tither or give offerings, they will object strenuously because, as we saw earlier, "All the preacher wants is your money."

You will not walk in the fullness of God's promises if you are shy about persecution. You should steel your spine as you embrace the truth that I am presenting to you, because many people who have no Scriptural knowledge and will not understand why you do it. Just don't let their persecution hinder you from applying it to your life. Just as I saw results, others in Scripture got results, and so will you.

When Jesus taught about the hindrances to receiving the seed of God's Word, He made it clear that persecution can steal truth from us. In Mark 4, Jesus reveals different types of soil. When one is not rooted and grounded in the Word of God, persecution will intimidate you. I am certain this is why the Spirit of God has mandated that I reduce this revelation to writing. It will assist you in becoming established in this truth and you will have an unshakeable conviction of giving honor to your spiritual leadership through tangible monetary gifts. Without being rooted, you will start doing this but not keep it going. Let's read what Jesus said about this.

> "And have no root in themselves, and so endure but for a time: afterward, when affliction or persecution ariseth for the word's sake, immediately they are offended." (Mark 4:17)

Some will challenge you about giving to your pastor because they see the quality of his or her life and think that they don't need it. Your gift does not have to be benevolence! Paul was very bold about the fact that he was not destitute or begging.

> "But I have all, and abound: I am full, having received of Epaphroditus the things which were sent from you, an odour of a sweet smell, a sacrifice acceptable, wellpleasing to God." (Philippians 4:18)

Some may even say that your pastor makes too much. Yet, how do you know what your shepherd makes? Could they have financial streams from other sources? Would you want someone to limit your ability to legally earn money for your family? Why would you limit someone who has sold out to God and given his or her life to His service? Wouldn't you want to follow someone who embodies not only the sacrifice, but also the surplus of obeying God?

When your objectors can't shake your commitment to give despite of the pastor's prosperity, they will attempt to impugn his or her integrity through innuendo, rumors and lies. This is an effort to decimate the pastor's holy standing in order to disqualify him or her from receiving financial support. You should never entertain an accusation against a shepherd without clear evidence from multiple witnesses. This is a Biblical standard to ensure that those in spiritual leadership are not maligned unnecessarily without due process.

> *"Do not receive an accusation against an elder except from two or three witnesses. Those who are sinning rebuke in the presence of all, that the rest also may fear. I charge you before God and the Lord Jesus Christ and the elect angels that you observe these things without prejudice, doing nothing with partiality." (1 Timothy 5:19-21)*

Those whom God has called to serve in ministry endure enough challenges of public life and scrutiny. They should not be subjected to unwarranted character assassination especially without meeting a Scriptural burden of proof. Do not allow someone to amplify the perceived imperfections of your leader to suggest some level of immorality, illegality, or ungodliness. If you don't know it for a fact, you must give leadership the benefit of the doubt.

The hallmark of a Biblical leader is that there is a commitment to good government, transparency, and financial accountability. You will never know all that is going on in your church. You will never see nor should you desire to see every transaction that your ministry makes. You should not expect to know your pastor's salary. What you should know is that there are clear policies and processes in place that enforce accountability. (We will get more into this in Section 5.) Without question, your pastor should be the leader of the ministry with flexibility to enact God's vision for the church and oversee the government of the ministry. This does not give license for a lack of accountability in handling church affairs, both civil authority, and Kingdom standards require accountability. Once you see these structures in place, give the ministry and your pastor, your total support and reject what "they say."

By all means, never participate in an unScriptural opposition against your pastor or spiritual leadership. We must be careful of using worldly attempts to manage God's church by secular behaviors. Even when there is blatant unrighteousness and the violation of civil laws, you must tread carefully. If your pastor is caught in a fault and submits to a restoration plan, you should remain silent and prayerful. It is a good thing that every pastor be submitted to an elder statesman (pastor), and board of directors or a pastoral organization. I often think it is important to put one's self in the place of another and ask, "How would I want to be treated in this type of situation?" You should really let the Words of Jesus guide you.

> *"And as ye would that men should do to you, do ye also to them likewise." (Luke 6:31)*

Don't think that because your pastor does not know you personally that they are unworthy of your financial seed. Because this is a spiritual relationship and you are living by a spiritual principle, the key is whether or not God sees! And, He does!

> *"For God is not unrighteous to forget your work and labour of love, which ye have shewed toward his name, in that ye have ministered to the saints, and do minister." (Hebrews 6:10)*

THE RESOLVE FOR GIVING HONOR

As you can imagine, when you are a financial blessing to your pastor, it is a great encouragement to his or her life. But, greater still, it is a blessing to your life. But, for a moment, I want you to gain an understanding of how your faithfulness to sow into spiritual leadership refreshes your man or woman of God. You will never know the multifaceted sacrifices that are made to serve in spiritual leadership, unless you walk in the shoes of someone in pastoral ministry. This refreshing does not just come from money alone. You will recall how I mentioned that true Biblical honor involved due and fitting recognition, respect, and resources. How often do you thank your pastor for the investments that he or she makes in your life? How often do you send a note of encouragement for a message or how the pastor handled a situation? Do you give cards on birthdays, anniversaries, and holidays? These are strategic times when you can inspire the one who inspires you! While I am always appreciative of every gift that is given to me, regardless of the size, I thoroughly enjoy reading cards and notes of appreciation. They minister to Pastor Bridget and me. I have been in ministry at this writing for over 50 years and yet a word of encouragement still refreshes me!

There is no downside to honoring your pastor! You just have to cultivate the resolve to continue to practice this with much joy and expectation of increase. When I first received this revelation, I saw quick results. I cannot say, for each time and season of my life that I have given, I have seen immediate manifested results. I continue to bless those in spiritual leadership who bless me because I know it honors others and pleases God.

Your resolve must be anchored in the Word of God. Your mind is the key to staying the course!

> *"I beseech you therefore, brethren, by the mercies of God, that ye present your bodies a living sacrifice, holy, acceptable unto God, which is your*

> *reasonable service. And be not conformed to this world: but be ye transformed by the renewing of your mind, that ye may prove what is that good, and acceptable, and perfect, will of God."*
> *(Romans 12:1-2)*

As you work this principle, you need to re-read this book and meditate on the Scriptures. Keep your eyes focused, like a laser, on the harvest you expect to receive. Your sowing into your pastor should be founded on a Scriptural promise that you expect to receive from your investment. This expectation should be set at a high level because you know that God will always go above your expectations.

> *"Now unto him that is able to do exceeding abundantly above all that we ask or think, according to the power that worketh in us, Unto him be glory in the church by Christ Jesus throughout all ages, world without end. Amen." (Ephesians 3:20-21)*

Your faith can only work based on fully persuaded expectations. So, how do you become fully persuaded?

It all starts with Deliberation. After reading to this section, take some time to consider the Biblical claims made in this book. Re-read the introduction and reflect on what God did supernaturally in my life. Know that God is not a respecter of persons. What He has done for me, He will do for you! This is a critical stage because you must evaluate what the Scripture teaches and weigh it against rumor and prejudices. If you will attest that the Bible is the truth of God's Word that we should live by, then you must conclude that this is the order of God.

Then there is Confirmation. You pursue these truths for yourself and set your will to believe. You do not place your faith in the testimony of others, only the testimony of Scripture. At this stage, you should craft a confession (verbal affirmation) in keeping with your Scriptural expectations. Confess something stated as follows.

CONFESSION OF FAITH

I believe the Word of God is truth and that God approves and is pleased when I honor my pastor. I thank You for the privilege to honor those who bless my life. I receive by faith the promises of Scripture of a first class life for my obedience.

Once you have this confession, you should remain faithful to say it daily (even multiple times daily). Don't discount making time to meditate on your expectations.

Next, is the Elimination stage. Survey your life to see if there are people that serve to contradict your faith expectations. If you are around negative people who don't believe in honoring Spiritual Leadership, you might consider redefining your relationship or placing guidelines that would insure you would not discuss this matter. Their poison will contaminate your faith and cause you frustration. I just want you to give God's Word a chance to work. It can't work if your friends and associates are constantly undermining your faith with negative talk and persecution. Are there other things in your life that diminish your expectations? Cut them off! You have too much at stake to jeopardize this process.

Now, it's time for Saturation. This is where you flood yourself with God's Word on this matter. Find teachings on honoring spiritual leadership from reputable Biblical teachers. Talk with like-minded people about this principle and the results that they have had in sowing into their pastor. Reflect about the manifestations you have seen thus far in sowing. You should be consumed with your pursuit of the supernatural lifestyle that your sowing has ignited. This level of inundation will ensure that you are not distracted by human logic or reasoning.

Saturation will inspire Consecration. You are completely submitted to pursuing God's will in this area. You see everything that you give to your man or woman of God as ministry. You sense that it is an honor and privilege to support God's servant. You must intercede regularly for your pastor. You continue to invest in your pastor systematically and spontaneously. You get involved in a service area and do it with all your heart. Lastly, you serve as a source of inspiration for moving forward. There are enough distractions and detours in ministry. You must be a cheerleader for the vision and the things of God; after all, your harvest is tied to its success. Remember that everything you are doing is for God's glory.

At this point, you are ready to step into the pursuit of God's plan and purposes that only a supernatural move can bring to pass. This is called Demonstration. You are acting as if the grace of your pastor is on your life. Things that were unthinkable and seemingly unattainable are now within your reach. You have a new grace flowing into your life. Just like Elisha had to act like he believed that his leader's grace was on him because of his faithfulness, so must we, because of our faithfulness. Situations that were previously unsuccessful will be turned around. The "No's" you received in the past will become "Yes." Rejoice and Act like it is so!

Lastly, you should be consumed with Celebration. Every day, praise God for this new level of grace and anointing that is on you. When obstacles rise, rejoice. If you receive a negative response, dance for joy because your deliverance draws nigh. Intentionally place a demand on your giving and service to your leader with your praise. Never let complaints come out of your mouth. Regardless of the circumstances, remain in an attitude of praise. This is a faith action that will bring forth the supernatural in the midst of seemingly insurmountable odds. If God has done it once, He will, and can, do it again!

Being fully persuaded is your key to manifestation! Do not overlook this process. Knowing that your pastor is good ground means nothing if you don't sow in order to tap into the grace on his or her life. Don't take this revelation lightly. By all means, do not just let this book sit on the shelf. This is your pathway to a supernatural life and lifestyle.

SECTION FOUR

The Character Correction - The Renegades

High-level honor seems to be a lost practice in our society. As we have overemphasized our individuality and our independence from others, we have abandoned respect for anyone other than ourselves. This is true in our culture and in the church. When I was growing up, there used to be a sense of respect for those who wore uniforms, were in elected office, served as officers in the church, or was the pastor. Over time, I have watched this erode where blatant acts of disrespect are allowed with impunity. I am not trying to paint a rosy portrait of the past because there were churches that were known for fighting the pastor, but overall, there was a greater sense of honor for those to whom honor was due.

THE DEVASTATING RETRIBUTION FOR DISHONOR

Now, there is a commonality today that no matter what your title or position, you are seen as just a man or a woman. You may have even heard people say, "Why would I give to him? He puts on his pants one leg at a time like I do." This is an unwise statement because in the process of honor, no one is negating the humanity of the person being honored. The honor is due out of deference to the office that the person occupies. The President of the United States puts on his pants one leg at a time as all people do. However, he can wear those pants into places that others cannot go. Moreover, he makes decisions that people are not capable of making who put on pants the same way he does. The office and the person in the office are always to be honored.

We would do well to remember Paul's admonition to the church in Rome.

> *"Let every soul be subject unto the higher powers. For there is no power but of God: the powers that be are ordained of God." (Romans 13:1)*

There is not another position more important on the earth than the Office of Pastor. As we have allowed secular and satanic influences to cloud our actions, we have given place to a stronghold against spiritual leadership. We must pull these down if we are to offer due and fitting respect, recognition and resources to God's servants.

The seeds have already been planted from the culture to dishonor one another and those in leadership. Have you ever noticed that you could be in a meeting and when someone leaves the room for a period of time, almost immediately, that person becomes the target of snide remarks or some type of negative words? And, the moment they return, there are smiles and warm welcomes as if nothing had ever been said. We have allowed a stronghold to develop which is keeping us from experiencing the supernatural dimension that God has promised. The good thing is that the devil is predictable and will always run the same game to lead you down the road to dishonor.

> *"Lest satan should get an advantage of us: for we are not ignorant of his devices."*
> *(2 Corinthians 2:11)*

Let's look at the ways in which satan deludes us into dishonor:

First, he feeds your mind unfounded derogatory thoughts to corrupt your commitment. Our mind, though a powerful force, can lead us down a road of suspicion and insinuation if left unchecked. You may observe an action by your spiritual leader, jump to unrighteous conclusions, and be quick to condemn and judge based on incomplete information, rather than follow the admonition of Philippians 4:8.

> *"Finally, brethren, whatsoever things are true, whatsoever things are honest, whatsoever things are just, whatsoever things are pure, whatsoever things are lovely, whatsoever things are of good report; if there be any virtue, and if there be any praise, think on these things." (Philippians 4:8)*

In other instances, someone may bring you accusatory, unconfirmed statements about your spiritual leaders that have planted a seed of doubt in your mind. Regardless of the delivery vehicle, the origin is satanic and designed to weaken your commitment to God's servant. The devil does not play fair. So, you will need to guard your heart to ensure that your righteous commitment is not corrupted. When the devil does this, it is only to stop the flow of the supernatural into your life. The devil knows what God has promised you and what is in store for your life if you honor spiritual leadership. So, if he can get you disconnected and pull back on your commitment, he will have halted, or at least delayed, the supernatural flow that God promised you based on this principle.

If the devil can't play with your mind, he will cause you to discount the grace factor that is transferred through your partnership with your man or woman of God. All of the devil ploys are subtle. If you start to feel you do not need someone to teach you, or if you entertain thoughts of independence from attending church and submitting to your pastor's vision, you should be careful because you could be under attack. Satan often uses the unwarranted feelings of dissatisfaction to blow believers off course. You learned earlier about the impartation of unstoppable grace that comes from your sowing. You may desire to have the testimony that you did it without the aid or assistance of another, but that is not God's way. Every person who has accomplished anything for God has done so by God's grace transferred through another. Our salvation came through Jesus. Moses' organization skills came through Jethro. Joshua's leadership came though Moses. Timothy's zeal to serve came through

Paul. It is the established order of God that you receive a grace impartation to accomplish what you have been assigned to do. Never discount the grace of another that you can be tapped into by your seed. When you discount the grace transference, you will forfeit the blessings and benefits that come from that connection. The grace is not only an empowerment to accomplish things; it also is your passport to the supernatural life! Many of the blessings you've been praying for would manifest if you would just stay connected to your spiritual leadership and walk in their grace. Scripture attests, you will forfeit new abilities and blessings by discounting the grace on your man or woman of God.

It is a logical progression, once the grace is discounted; offense takes place that will cause a disconnection from the local church. Because of offense or disappointment, so many people have chosen to stop attending church and even communing with God one on one. If you are reading this book today and that is the position you have taken, I want to lovingly say to you that you have been deceived. I am not minimizing what you have gone through, but it is not God's best for you to be disconnected from His church. When you have stopped going to church, you have willingly stepped out of God's ordained path for your life. God set you in His body as it pleased Him. (1 Corinthians 12:18) In essence, you have benched yourself from the battle and you are on the sidelines. You cannot fulfill your purpose by sitting at home watching ministry on television or over the Internet. You exist for the benefit of another!

> *"For we are his workmanship, created in Christ Jesus unto good works, which God hath before ordained that we should walk in them."*
> *(Ephesians 2:10)*

Your faith in Christ is lived out among the saints in Church and in the world as an ambassador for Christ. Let me remind you of what the Bible says.

> *"And let us consider one another in order to stir up love and good works, not forsaking the assembling of ourselves together, as is the manner of some, but exhorting one another, and so much the more as you see the Day approaching."*
> *(Hebrews 10:24-24)*

Get back in the game and finish strong what God has given you to do. Confess forgiveness over past situations and reclaim your place in the local church where God set you.

Next, the devil will attempt to persuade you that you are being held back and can do better by yourself. This is very similar to discounting the grace factor except that you feel that you have so much more to offer and your gifts are not being utilized as you feel they should be. Notice how many times the word "feel" was used in that previous sentence? The devil will exploit your feelings to walk away from the place that God set you. Remember the devil has been exposed to your future. Just when you are ready to walk into your new level, he will get you off track and miss an opportunity. I have seen this too many times in my ministry. I can remember when there was a young man that I sensed could assume a new level of ministry at my church. I had watched him grow and develop and I was almost ready to make the announcement. Just when I had made the decision, he started to feel underutilized and unappreciated. He subsequently left the ministry and to this day has not fulfilled what God called him to do. He was so close to getting everything that he had prayed for and expected, but he walked away prematurely.

Gehazi had faithfully served Elisha. And, one day, after Naaman was healed of his leprosy, Elisha turned away the generosity of Naaman. Gehazi thought this was inappropriate and concocted a plan or dishonor to get that offering for himself.

> "But Gehazi, the servant of Elisha the man of God, said, Behold, my master hath spared Naaman this Syrian, in not receiving at his hands that which he brought: but, as the LORD liveth, I will run after him, and take somewhat of him. So Gehazi followed after Naaman. And when Naaman saw him running after him, he lighted down from the chariot to meet him, and said, Is all well? And he said, All is well. My master hath sent me, saying, Behold, even now there be come to me from mount Ephraim two young men of the sons of the prophets: give them, I pray thee, a talent of silver, and two changes of garments. And Naaman said, Be content, take two talents. And he urged him, and bound two talents

> of silver in two bags, with two changes of garments, and laid them upon two of his servants; and they bare them before him. And when he came to the tower, he took them from their hand, and bestowed them in the house: and he let the men go, and they departed. But he went in, and stood before his master. And Elisha said unto him, Whence comest thou, Gehazi? And he said, Thy servant went no whither. And he said unto him, Went not mine heart with thee, when the man turned again from his chariot to meet thee? Is it a time to receive money, and to receive garments, and oliveyards, and vineyards, and sheep, and oxen, and menservants, and maidservants? The leprosy therefore of Naaman shall cleave unto thee, and unto thy seed for ever. And he went out from his presence a leper as white as snow." (2 Kings 5:20-27)

I never stop passing along this piece of wisdom I received more than 3 decades ago, "You can make a blessing and you'll miss a blessing; and, the blessing you miss will be greater than the blessing you made." I see people making blessings for themselves who have authentic calls on their lives. Oh, they may flourish for a while, but it is still far less than what God had predestined for them! Stay in your set place. Have a conversation with your pastor about your future. Get regular feedback about your performance and areas where you should grow. Fight the feelings of frustration for being underutilized. Trust your pastor to know when you are ready; after all, they have treaded the path that you are pursuing. They see more than you think that they can. Trust the process.

Because some are in fear of being "held back" by their leaders, they wander aimlessly throughout the Body of Christ going from one church to another, never staying longer than their first "no" response. If you postpone making your Kingdom connection with spiritual leadership and remain disconnected, you will miss God's promotional plan. Promotion comes from God through people and, as a result of your faithfulness.

> "He that is faithful in that which is least is faithful also in much: and he that is unjust in the least is unjust also in much. If therefore ye have not been faithful in the unrighteous mammon, who will commit to your trust the true riches? And if ye have not been faithful in that which is another man's, who shall give you that which is your own?" (Luke 16:10-12)

God uses your faithfulness to another person's vision to position you for what He has in store for you. If you cannot remain consistently committed to someone else, how will you ever be ready to lead your own ministry? The apprenticeship factor is real. Why abort the training process so that you can go out into ministry and make common mistakes that your training could have prevented? More is caught than taught. Being near your pastor and following him or her will show you how to handle situations in life and ministry. You may assume that you know more than your pastor does and in some areas, you may. But, God did not send you to that pastor for what you knew, but for what you do not know. Trust the fruit of your pastor's ministry to give you hope that your time will come because it will.

You must have the strength of character not to attempt to take a perceived short cut paved by betrayal. You must trust the process of integrity and faithfulness. Years ago, as a young preacher, my Pastor, and mentor would allow one of the church's singing group to accompany me when I would go out to preach. It was definitely an asset to me because when other pastors knew that a crowd would be following me, I became a young preacher in demand.

After one outing, several of the singing group leaders came to me and offered a proposition. They said that if I would start a church, they would all go with me because they all enjoyed my preaching. It was an underhanded move from them to entice me to go against my pastor and ultimately attempt to split the church. Of course, you know I turned them down and told them I was going to report them to the pastor. I reported them and my Pastor and Father in the Faith appreciated my loyalty. He reprimanded them and would not allow them to travel with me anymore. It was a bittersweet episode, but through it, I maintained my integrity!

Often, I am asked about the perceived success that those who have betrayed their spiritual leaders seem to be experiencing.

One pastor suggested that it looks appealing when successfully splitting a church where they served. By simply asking the Lord and the Pastor for forgiveness, you can move on keeping the members who left with you and go on with the acceptance of the community.

First, you cannot assume that there are no consequences when rebellion takes place. In fact, it's quite the controversy. God is not to be mocked, you will reap what you sow; further, what looks like Kingdom success, many times is just the product of what human talent and skill can produce. I would not risk the favor of God by gambling with rebellion and betrayal to get ahead in life. Remember, rebellion is equal to witchcraft and opens the door to satanic encroachment, which could prove most regrettable.

Let me ask you, "What are your motives?" This is a real question because if you want to walk in this supernatural life, your motives must be pure. Situations evoking patience are great ways that God uses to check your motives. Are you really in your set place to serve or biding your time until something better comes along? If your motives are perverted, you will end up betraying your pastor. This happened to Judas. We all know that Judas betrayed Jesus, but do you know why?

> "And being in Bethany in the house of Simon the leper, as he sat at meat, there came a woman having an alabaster box of ointment of spikenard very precious; and she brake the box, and poured

> it on his head. And there were some that had indignation within themselves, and said, 'Why was this waste of the ointment made? For it might have been sold for more than three hundred pence, and have been given to the poor.' And they murmured against her. And Jesus said, 'Let her alone; why trouble ye her? she hath wrought a good work on me. For ye have the poor with you always, and whensoever ye will ye may do them good: but me ye have not always. She hath done what she could: she is come aforehand to anoint my body to the burying. Verily I say unto you, Wheresoever this Gospel shall be preached throughout the whole world, this also that she hath done shall be spoken of for a memorial of her.' And Judas Iscariot, one of the twelve, went unto the chief priests, to betray him unto them." (Mark 14:3-10)

On the heels of a public rebuke from Jesus, this challenged the motives of the Disciples; the Bible records that Judas set his betrayal plan in motion. John 12:3-8 gives greater clarity.

> "Then took Mary a pound of ointment of spikenard, very costly, and anointed the feet of Jesus, and wiped his feet with her hair: and the house was filled with the odour of the ointment. Then saith one of his disciples, Judas Iscariot, Simon's son, which should betray him, 'Why was not this ointment sold for three hundred pence, and given to the poor?' This he said, not that he cared for the poor; but

> *because he was a thief, and had the bag, and bare what was put therein.* Then said Jesus, 'Let her alone: against the day of my burying hath she kept this. *For the poor always ye have with you; but me ye have not always.*' " (John 12:3-8)

Betrayal is always linked to a moment in time when an offense or disappointment has occurred. Rather than properly process the situation, you internalize the negative emotions and set your course towards betrayal. There is a window, albeit a small one, where you can check these emotions. If not, you will destroy the Kingdom connection that God has brought into your life. And, just like Judas, when the story is told in the future, you will be a byline and the one you sought to betray will still be center stage. God never honors betrayal. If you have a legitimate concern with your pastor, you should schedule a meeting and talk! Work through all the issues in private and seek to maintain the relationship. Never think that God sanctions betrayal because it is not God.

Here are some other signs of a perverted motive. Do you have a toxic attitude? Are you mentally challenging every word from your pastor? Are you seething with resentment below the surface? Are you completing tasks in a half-hearted manner? Quiet as it may be kept, your attitude does show in your actions—even in facial expressions.

You may also have the symptoms of a perverted motive if you are rewriting your testimony and leaving out people who helped you. If a person's investment in your life was meaningful at the time, then why has offense cancelled out that deposit? Your life is the sum total of the investments that have been made into you. These you cannot obliterate. I call this testimonial amnesia.

I grew up in the Baptist Church denomination and later became an Independent. I have been careful to give honor to all the mentors and Fathers in the Faith that poured into my life over those years. It is the only right thing to do because it is the truth. I learned so much about life, ministry, and pastoring long before embracing the Word of Faith.

Have you intentionally forgotten the impact others have made in your life? This is dangerous because that which you do to another will most certainly come back to you. Those whom you have helped will rise up one day and replicate your bad behavior. To deny someone's deposit in your life is an affront to God because He placed that person in your life.

Still others practice what I call timely absenteeism as a means to show their perverted motives. Not every absence is innocuous. Some people use their nonattendance to send a clear signal that they are not with the vision. Empty chairs do tell a story. In this case, it tells a nefarious story of one whose heart is polluted and waiting to strike. To those who are faithful, these timely absences speak volumes! Don't think that there are excuses, which can cover this undercover rebellion, because it cannot. When you should be in place and you are not, a message is being sent!

Most importantly, this message is to God, which says, you are not ready for your next level!

Lastly, a perverted motive is manifested through talking assassins. This is the most blatant display of rebellion. To anyone who will listen, you actively tell lies and mischaracterizations in order to bolster your insurgence. Why do people think that God respects tearing down one of His servants—or any person for that matter? It is important to see what the Bible says about this destructive behavior.

> "These six things the LORD hates, Yes, seven are an abomination to Him: A proud look, a lying tongue, and hands that shed innocent blood."
> (Proverbs 6:16-17)

> "He who has a deceitful heart finds no good, And he who has a perverse tongue falls into evil."
> (Proverbs 17:20)

> "Whoever guards his mouth and tongue Keeps his soul from troubles. A proud and haughty man-- "Scoffer" is his name; He acts with arrogant pride."
> (Proverbs 21:23-24)

> "Even so the tongue is a little member and boasts great things. See how great a forest a little fire kindles! And the tongue is a fire, a world of iniquity. The tongue is so set among our members that it

> defiles the whole body, and sets on fire the course of nature; and it is set on fire by hell." (James 3:5-6)

This is a small sampling of the Scriptures that show God's disdain for verbal assaults on people. All of these evil words are birthed out of an offended heart.

> "A good man out of the good treasure of his heart bringeth forth that which is good; and an evil man out of the evil treasure of his heart bringeth forth that which is evil: for of the abundance of the heart his mouth speaketh." (Luke 6:45)

Talking assassins are self-destructive and their words will be an end to them! I have spent the last several pages exposing these bad behaviors because I want every person who reads this book to walk in the supernatural flow of abundant provisions. You can sow your seed and service and still will not see a harvest because your rebellious acts of dishonor cancel your seed. The grace transfer is cancelled out. If any of this represented a behavior in which you engage, repent now. Cancel out every negative word. Repent to your man or woman of God. Get back on track so that you can walk in the unstoppable grace of God! Then, you can see the dynamic rewards from honor.

THE DYNAMIC REWARDS FOR DISCIPLINED HONOR

How intensely do you desire to see the promised Scriptural harvest manifest in your life? You will recall that there are significant benefits to those who will honor their pastor with tangible financial gifts. If you will establish a disciplined regimen of honor, you will release this flow into your life. Discipline is enforced obedience. Now that you have seen this Scriptural, spiritual principle, it requires a self-restraint to practice it consistently.

When you release honor with your monetary gift, a spiritual momentum is sparked. This momentum is the force that is released into the earth as a result of obedience, which attracts an ever-increasing participation of both spiritual and natural assistance to overcome obstacles to accomplish the will of God. This undeniable and unstoppable favor of God makes this principle powerful. When I first learned about honoring spiritual leadership, I had a decision to make, "Would I faithfully follow it or overlook its truth?" My life had been transformed because of this principle. I have shown myself faithful to every spiritual leader whom God placed in my life. My father always cautioned me never to waste someone's time who seeks to make an investment in my life.

That first $5 offering into my pastor's life started a spiritual momentum that has kept me. This is why you should not delay to enact this principle because the sooner you get started, the more momentum you will gain, and the longer that spiritual momentum runs, the more harvest you will see. When I have wanted to hear a Word from God, I have intentionally practiced this principle and God has spoken.

There has been several occasions when I needed wisdom in a

particular area and I sensed the leading of the Lord to sow into a particular mentor. I have always obeyed and God has always showed up with the wisdom I needed.

The harvest is worth making the necessary changes in your life. In addition to overcoming the negative emotions that keep you from sowing, you should also pull down any religious or carnal strongholds that could work against you.

> "For though we walk in the flesh, we do not war after the flesh: (For the weapons of our warfare are not carnal, but mighty through God to the pulling down of strong holds;) Casting down imaginations, and every high thing that exalteth itself against the knowledge of God, and bringing into captivity every thought to the obedience of Christ; And having in a readiness to revenge all disobedience, when your obedience is fulfilled."
> (2 Corinthians 10:3-6)

You will need to break free from all emotional strongholds and birth emotional strength. Have you been conditioned to erroneously think that every preacher who makes a financial appeal is "running a game on you?" You may have some strongholds that need to be attacked. However, you will never get to the level of disciplined performance, if you just clean out emotional baggage. You will also have to cultivate emotional fortitude to maintain consistency even under persecution.

Your disciplined practice of honor will ignite a passion within you that cannot be quenched. As you see results from giving to your pastor, you will continue to do it aggressively! Harvest is always assured to the one who persistently works the process of faith.

> *"Cast not away therefore your confidence, which hath great recompence of reward. For ye have need of patience, that, after ye have done the will of God, ye might receive the promise." (Hebrews 10:35-36)*

> *"And we desire that every one of you do shew the same diligence to the full assurance of hope unto the end: That ye be not slothful, but followers of them who through faith and patience inherit the promises." (Hebrews 6:12)*

> *"But that on the good ground are they, which in an honest and good heart, having heard the word, keep it, and bring forth fruit with patience." (Luke 8:15)*

Here are some examples of those who passionately pursued harvest. The common trait is that they all received what they pursued.

THE STORY OF BLIND BARTIMAEUS

> *"And they came to Jericho: and as he went out of*

> Jericho with his disciples and a great number of people, blind Bartimaeus, the son of Timaeus, sat by the highway side begging. And when he heard that it was Jesus of Nazareth, he began to cry out, and say, Jesus, thou Son of David, have mercy on me. And many charged him that he should hold his peace: but he cried the more a great deal, Thou Son of David, have mercy on me. And Jesus stood still, and commanded him to be called. And they call the blind man, saying unto him, Be of good comfort, rise; he calleth thee. And he, casting away his garment, rose, and came to Jesus. And Jesus answered and said unto him, What wilt thou that I should do unto thee? The blind man said unto him, Lord, that I might receive my sight. And Jesus said unto him, Go thy way; thy faith hath made thee whole. And immediately he received his sight, and followed Jesus in the way." (Mark 10:46-52)

THE STORY OF THE SYROPHONECIAN WOMAN

> "But he answered her not a word. And his disciples came and besought him, saying, Send her away; for she crieth after us. But he answered and said, I am not sent but unto the lost sheep of the house of Israel. Then came she and worshipped him, saying, Lord, help me. But he answered and said, It is not meet to take the children's bread, and to cast it to dogs. And she said, Truth, Lord: yet the dogs eat of the crumbs which fall from their masters' table. Then Jesus answered and said unto her, O woman,

great is thy faith: be it unto thee even as thou wilt. And her daughter was made whole from that very hour." (Matthew 15:23-28)

THE STORY OF A FATHER WHOSE SON WAS POSSESSED

"And when they were come to the multitude, there came to him a certain man, kneeling down to him, and saying, Lord, have mercy on my son: for he is lunatick, and sore vexed: for ofttimes he falleth into the fire, and oft into the water. And I brought him to thy disciples, and they could not cure him. Then Jesus answered and said, O faithless and perverse generation, how long shall I be with you? how long shall I suffer you? bring him hither to me. And Jesus rebuked the devil; and he departed out of him: and the child was cured from that very hour. Then came the disciples to Jesus apart, and said, Why could not we cast him out? And Jesus said unto them, Because of your unbelief: for verily I say unto you, If ye have faith as a grain of mustard seed, ye shall say unto this mountain, Remove hence to yonder place; and it shall remove; and nothing shall be impossible unto you."
(Matthew 17:14-20)

You will control the harvest that you receive by how you tenaciously apply the truth you have learned. Pastor Bridget and I are living witnesses that sowing into spiritual leadership works. Drive out all unbelief and negative mental strongholds and you will experience abundance that you could have only dreamed.

Start today by correcting your character and implementing this principle faithfully. Harvest is assured!

SECTION FIVE

The Corporate Commitment - The Responsibility

I am providing this section to further educate you as to the comprehensive recognition system that your ministry should have in place for your pastor. Please know that I am not a lawyer and this in no way is meant to offer you counsel beyond spiritual wisdom that I have gained over the years.

By now, you know that it is very much a Biblical truth that the pastor should be supported by those whom he or she serves. In Old Testament practice, God established a priestly order whose needs were met by the children of Israel.

> *"In the most holy place shalt thou eat it; every male shall eat it: it shall be holy unto thee. And this is thine; the heave offering of their gift, with all the wave offerings of the children of Israel: I have given them unto thee, and to thy sons and to thy daughters with thee, by a statute for ever: every one that is clean in thy house shall eat of it. All the best of the oil, and all the best of the wine, and of the wheat, the firstfruits of them which they shall offer unto the LORD, them have I given thee. And whatsoever is*

first ripe in the land, which they shall bring unto the LORD, shall be thine; every one that is clean in thine house shall eat of it. Every thing devoted in Israel shall be thine. Every thing that openeth the matrix in all flesh, which they bring unto the LORD, whether it be of men or beasts, shall be thine: nevertheless the firstborn of man shalt thou surely redeem, and the firstling of unclean beasts shalt thou redeem. And those that are to be redeemed from a month old shalt thou redeem, according to thine estimation, for the money of five shekels, after the shekel of the sanctuary, which is twenty gerahs. But the firstling of a cow, or the firstling of a sheep, or the firstling of a goat, thou shalt not redeem; they are holy: thou shalt sprinkle their blood upon the altar, and shalt burn their fat for an offering made by fire, for a sweet savour unto the LORD. And the flesh of them shall be thine, as the wave breast and as the right shoulder are thine. All the heave offerings of the holy things, which the children of Israel offer unto the LORD, have I given thee, and thy sons and thy daughters with thee, by a statute for ever: it is a covenant of salt for ever before the LORD unto thee and to thy seed with thee. And the LORD spake unto Aaron, Thou shalt have no inheritance in their land, neither shalt thou have any part among them: I am thy part and thine inheritance among the children of Israel. And, behold, I have given the children of Levi all the tenth in Israel for an inheritance, for their service which they serve, even the service of the tabernacle of the congrega-

> tion. Neither must the children of Israel henceforth come nigh the tabernacle of the congregation, lest they bear sin, and die. But the Levites shall do the service of the tabernacle of the congregation, and they shall bear their iniquity: it shall be a statute for ever throughout your generations, that among the children of Israel they have no inheritance. But the tithes of the children of Israel, which they offer as an heave offering unto the LORD, I have given to the Levites to inherit: therefore I have said unto them, Among the children of Israel they shall have no inheritance." (Numbers 18:10-24)

We do well to remember that as God established worship practices, He included support for those who served Him in ministry! Your pastor is a professional and should be treated as one by the church. It should be evident in the way that the ministry cares for its pastor in regards to salary and benefits. You should be aware of the professional standard of compensating your pastor, as well as the Scriptural significance of compensating your pastor. In this way, when asked to participate, you can do so with the wisdom of God and a pure heart.

Whether it is through regular compensation or special days of recognition, you should see the giving of financial blessings to your pastor as a source of ministry to him or her. Let's see how Paul saw those who gave to him.

> *"For as touching the ministering to the saints, it is superfluous for me to write to you: For I know the forwardness of your mind, for which I boast of you to them of Macedonia, that Achaia was ready a year ago; and your zeal hath provoked very many. Yet have I sent the brethren, lest our boasting of you should be in vain in this behalf; that, as I said, ye may be ready: Lest haply if they of Macedonia come with me, and find you unprepared, we (that we say not, ye) should be ashamed in this same confident boasting. Therefore I thought it necessary to exhort the brethren, that they would go before unto you, and make up beforehand your bounty, whereof ye had notice before, that the same might be ready, as a matter of bounty, and not as of covetousness."* (2 Corinthians 9:1-5)

Paul encouraged his churches how to prepare to give towards his ministry. Thus, it is right for me to instruct you in specific ways that your church can bless its pastor.

Paul's conviction to teach his churches how to honor him was rooted in his firm belief that when you are in the service of another, you should not have to pay your own way.

> *"Who goeth a warfare any time at his own charges? who planteth a vineyard, and eateth not of the fruit thereof? or who feedeth a flock, and eateth not of the milk of the flock? Say I these things as a man? or saith not the law the same also? For it is written*

> in the law of Moses, Thou shalt not muzzle the mouth of the ox that treadeth out the corn. Doth God take care for oxen? Or saith he it altogether for our sakes? For our sakes, no doubt, this is written: that he that ploweth should plow in hope; and that he that thresheth in hope should be partaker of his hope. If we have sown unto you spiritual things, is it a great thing if we shall reap your carnal things?"
> (1 Corinthians 9:7-11)

Based on Scripture, your church has an obligation to reasonably compensate your pastor so that he or she can perform their calling unencumbered. God expects that you will also personally do what you can to bless your pastor. Let's get to the nuts and bolts of pastoral compensation and recognition.

COMPETITIVE COMPENSATION

Your pastor should receive a salary commensurate with the expertise he or she possesses. This expertise comes in the form of years of experience, training, certifications, degrees, and the like. Salary should also take into account the scope of responsibility that that pastor has. Most people think the pastor only works on Sunday! They do not take into account that the pastor is on call for emergencies, counsels people in distress, performs sacerdotal duties, and administrates the church. The public ministry aspect of the role is very limited to the larger scope of the pastor's full responsibilities. Your pastor's compensation plan should include merit salary increases for ability and experience in addition to cost of living increases. To better assess the fair compensation for a pastor, and comply with Internal Revenue Regulations, your church should have an external compensation study performed to set a reasonable benchmark for the pastor's complete compensation package. But, the foundation of all compensation is the salary. Also, your pastor is legally entitled to other benefits.

HEALTH INSURANCE

Pastors should have health insurance offered by the church, so that they can have access to medical services when they are needed. Moreover, because of the level of responsibility that pastors carry, there are many preventative options available for screenings and tests. Because pastors are professionals, having in place a solid health insurance plan will allow the pastor's family to have the assurance of good health maintenance.

LIFE INSURANCE

Your pastor is a key person in the ministry and as such, his or her sudden and unexpected death could interrupt the efficient and effective flow of the ministry. There are key man insurance policies available that allow the pastor's family and the church to share in the payout from the policy. You should target the minimum policy at $1,000,000. From the church's portion, the pastor can receive a dignified funeral and provide for resources for the church as it transitions to the new pastor. (While I did not cover it completely in this book, each church, especially independent churches, should have a succession plan in place, which covers all eventualities.) The family portion will enable them to continue living and make a transition as well. Many do not fully understand the sacrifices that pastor's families make and in the unlikely event that the pastor passes, the family may not have a means to continue to receive compensation outside of ministry. In addition to this policy, the pastor should have a policy that names his or her family as the sole beneficiary.

RETIREMENT

Your pastor should have a comprehensive retirement account so that when he or she is ready to transition out of active pastoral ministry, a plan is in place for the transition. One's retirement preparation should consist of salary replacement, housing accommodations, and resources to continue to function in ministry, after the pastoral role has ended. It is not Biblical to assume that a pastor will remain in office until they pass or leave ministry only to sit on a porch and do nothing. The call to ministry is full time. As I have always said, we clock in, but we do not clock out until we hear, "Well done, good and faithful servant." This is not to say that one should remain in pulpit ministry permanently. It means that at some point, the pastor should plan an orderly exit from pastoral ministry and transition into another ministry role. Even as I write this, I am executing our 7-year transition plan, which will take me from an active pastoral role to an itinerant ministry. Retirement for ministry has a different connotation, than for other professions. Thus, the normal rule for replacing only a portion of one's salary is not accurate. Retirement plans should produce equal to or greater funds to ensure that the person can operate independently and continue ministry.

PARSONAGE/HOUSING ALLOWANCE

One of the unique benefits afforded those in ministry is a parsonage or stipend for housing. Years ago, it was the norm to have a parsonage located on church property, where the pastor lived. Over the years, more ministries have opted for a housing allowance, which allows the pastor to live wherever he or she desires. The pastor receives an allowance that pays for the fair market value of the rent/mortgage payment and all household expenses including utilities, property taxes, insurance, maintenance, and upkeep. There is a form that is filled out annually, which lists these expenses and the allowance cannot exceed these. This benefit is important because it can even include expenses relative to relocation by providing funds for down payments. Housing allowances are the preferred way to provide lodging for pastors and their families because it enables them to procure an asset that their family can own. This gives a greater sense of stability and security for those serving in ministry.

REIMBURSEMENT FOR MINISTRY EXPENSE

The pastor should not have to come out of his or her pocket to pay expenses that are legitimately the ministry's expense. For instance, if the pastor takes staff out to eat, or buys pizza for the youth group, these are ministry expenses for which reimbursement is made. Every church should have a policy in place that allows for ministry expenses that are made by individuals in the church to be paid back without tax consequence. Many churches provide a corporate credit card to handle these expenses and it is most appropriate to do so.

CAR ALLOWANCE

Transportation is a requirement for ministry. From off-site meetings, travel to conferences, and visitation, pastors must have a reliable vehicle to carry out his or her assigned duties. Offering a church-owned vehicle or providing an allowance to compensate the pastor for church use of a private vehicle can meet this need. To be sure, the vehicle should be that which the church can afford.

EDUCATIONAL ALLOWANCE

Your pastor must stay on the cutting edge through constant training. A fund should be established which will facilitate attendance at seminars, workshops, specialized training, and even continuing education classes. Education is not optional for ministry. There is no professional discipline that does not require some sort of refreshing or exposure to new concepts. The same is true in ministry. If your pastor were restricted from pursuing these opportunities for personal growth, the church would have unknowingly stunted its own growth because the church will never grow beyond its leader. It should excite you when your pastor leaves for conferences, workshops, or seminars. It means that he or she is growing and you can expect that the church will grow as well.

SPECIAL RECOGNITION DAYS

You have already seen that it is most proper to give due and fitting respect, recognition and resources to your pastor. Due and fitting recognition can come in many forms and none of them are extraneous. Your annual church calendar must include times where the church turns aside to appreciate the role and function of your pastor. In the United States, October has been designated as clergy appreciation month. During this month, you will bless your pastor by giving a card with a financial gift included.

However, your recognition does not and in fact, should not, be limited to October. Many churches establish an annual appreciation for pastors that are most honorable. On these days, the pastor is recognized for significant accomplishments, special offerings are given, and professional perks. This teaches the coming generations, by example.

Here are some dates that you should know for your pastor and actively remember them with an appropriate gift. Your pastor's (and spouse's) birthday, wedding anniversary, Christmas, and even Easter are all great times to highlight your pastor's role in your life. While most people are enjoying these holidays, your pastor is on duty. Your conscious act of love and appreciation around these times will most certainly minister to him or her. In addition, you do not even have to limit your generosity to those times. As you reflect upon the role your pastor plays in your life and development, there is nothing wrong with spontaneously offering gifts of appreciation. One principle that I have operated with is that whenever I received income, I gave to my pastor. I know this has triggered supernatural blessings in my life.

Your pastor carries an enormous responsibility that may not be apparent to you. Every act of kindness is appreciated. Many pastors are prone to burn out from balancing so many responsibilities, and trying to meet the ever-increasing expectations of people. Pastors care for your soul. If they minister to you their spiritual things, shouldn't you be willing to minister to them your natural things?

The key that I want to convey to you is that whenever you are led to show appreciation by giving financial support to your pastor, you should do it unashamedly and boldly because you are positioning your life for exponential blessings.

There is so much more that can and should be said about pastoral compensation, but this section was designed to give you a broad overview of all the options available in order to treat your shepherd as the professional they are. This will ensure that you do not have an inferior church.

THE DIVINE RESTORATION FOR THE DISGRACED

In our day and age, we cannot talk about honoring God's servants without recognizing the painful effects of those who hold positions of trust and abuse, those placed in their care through covert sin and unrighteousness or perverted, predatory actions. While these are still a very small minority, the public effects of their misbehavior resound throughout the Body of Christ and secular society. While no leader is perfect, there is a justifiable expectation that pastors live by the Biblical code of conduct called holiness. Let me be clear; a person can serve in ministry for a lifetime and never experience public shame and humiliation, so long as he or she has a vibrant relationship with Jesus, viable accountability and visible transparency.

Leaders are not perfect; they may not make all the right management decisions, they may mishear the voice of God; and, they may be too impulsive when implementing vision. These mistakes are common on the path to becoming a great leader. When a spiritual leader has made one of these mistakes, it is imperative to disclose it and move forward. No leader should claim infallibility in decisions because we make the best decisions with the information we have available.

I recall early on in ministry, we purchased a piece of property as a church. We had poured a great deal of expense into this land and we were preparing to build to the glory of God. It just seemed that everything we tried to do with this land, failed. At one point, I thought the land was cursed! We would cut the grass one day and by the next day, it looked like it needed to be cut again. After a period of time, trying to make something work, I consulted with God about this situation. He clearly told me that it was not His will to build on that land. I was shocked because I had already told the people that I had heard from God. At that moment, I had to make a decision. Do I preserve my ego and infallibility or tell the people that I made a mistake.

Trusting and trembling, after the next Sunday morning

service, we dismissed all the guests and I explained to the church that I missed it. God did not want us to build on that land and we were going to sell it to recover all of our investment. I can still recall how nervous I was to stand before the people as a young preacher and tell them I made a mistake. Right after I finished apologizing to the church, one of my members yelled out, "We love you, Pastor!" As you can imagine, tears started to flow throughout the church. I recovered from that and have never made that mistake twice. We have since built or acquired over one million square feet of facilities and 500 acres of land. God will always honor us when we admit when we are at fault. You will never lose by admitting to making a leadership mistake.

Mistakes are very different from sin. Sin is a transgression against God and His Word. It literally means to go against God. God has no tolerance for sin and when one sins, something dies. When a person stops growing spiritually, and has no accountability or oversight, a sinful fall is inevitable! According to the Word of God, no person has to fall. Sin is a choice. You can choose not to sin!

> *"According as his divine power hath given unto us all things that pertain unto life and godliness, through the knowledge of him that hath called us to glory and virtue: Whereby are given unto us exceeding great and precious promises: that by these ye might be partakers of the divine nature, having escaped the corruption that is in the world*

> *through lust. And beside this, giving all diligence, add to your faith virtue; and to virtue knowledge; And to knowledge temperance; and to temperance patience; and to patience godliness; And to godliness brotherly kindness; and to brotherly kindness charity. For if these things be in you, and abound, they make you that ye shall neither be barren nor unfruitful in the knowledge of our Lord Jesus Christ. But he that lacketh these things is blind, and cannot see afar off, and hath forgotten that he was purged from his old sins. Wherefore the rather, brethren, give diligence to make your calling and election sure: for if ye do these things, ye shall never fall." (2 Peter 1:3-10)*

If one were maturing in the grace of God, the desire to sin and violate His mercy would be non-existent. Many will see a spiritual leader slipping and remain silent. If sin is concealed, it will be revealed. This is a fact. Don't trust your cover-up plan.

So, when a leader has been exposed and has repented, it is our responsibility to extend mercy. As a culture, we are quick to judge and throw people away. Yet, we would never want someone to do this to us. If you are facing a situation, where your spiritual leader has confessed and repented of a sin, then we who are spiritual should assist in the restoration.

> *"Brethren, if a man be overtaken in a fault, ye which are spiritual, restore such an one in the spirit of meekness; considering thyself, lest thou also be*

> tempted. Bear ye one another's burdens, and so fulfil the law of Christ. For if a man think himself to be something, when he is nothing, he deceiveth himself." (Galatians 6:1-3)

> "We then that are strong ought to bear the infirmities of the weak, and not to please ourselves." (Romans 15:1)

Never withhold mercy from another as an exercise of your power over them. It is a mistake to think that a recipient of mercy will continue to commit the same sin. It is also a mistake to think that extending mercy cancels all consequences. Mercy only cancels judgment nothing else. When you extend mercy to your pastor who has fallen, you send him or her a message that you have faith in them, forgive them and are willing to participate in their plan for recovery. You will also show God that you are worthy of mercy when you need it.

When a leader requires restoration, the first step is visible submission to an established model of integrity. This model of integrity may be a person or a panel of people. Their primary role is to assess the damage and assemble a restoration plan for the person. Accountability is a necessary element of any restoration plan. When sin has been public, the plan for restoration should be as well. In other words, those who are following the leader should know what is the restoration plan and even be updated from time to time on the process. This will re-establish trust as people publically observe the fallen leader being restored. Next, the leader requires time. This may require stopping all public ministry for a period of intense scrutiny, character evaluation, and spiritual refocusing. When a leader has publicly broken the trust with those whom he or she serves, it will take time to build that trust up again. Always remember that forgiveness is automatic, but trust must be earned!

Thirdly, re-entry into public ministry should be supervised for a period of time. There is no magic bullet in the restoration process. Once the restoration process has been completed, that is just phase one. I spent over a decade helping men and women break free from the bonds of addiction. One thing is certain is the initial restoration process is only one-step. It is a good step, but only one-step. There needs to be constant monitoring, mentoring, and meetings to ensure that the person stays on track with the commitments that were made during the rehabilitation process. At the point of re-entry into public ministry, the new accountability structures should be in place and publicly visible to give the sense that assistance is still available. Over a period of time, as the pastor holds his or her course, the pain of the failing will be erased from people's minds.

I am presenting this to help those reading this. In no way, is this meant to condemn someone who has fallen into sin. I have stood by many pastors who have breached the trust of their members; they submitted to the process, and I have seen them turn around their situation. You can do the same if you are dealing with hidden sins. Please do not trust your cover-up plan because as I mentioned above, it will fail! Trust God's process to forgive and restore you. That same grace that you have preached to others is available to you.

Showing mercy does not necessarily mean that the consequences are waived; the severity of the offense may mean that the people can no longer minister in that setting anymore. This does not negate the calling on the person's life but for the greater good of the ministry, separation may be appropriate. The person or panel who is charged with establishing the restoration plan would determine this. Tough love sometimes means that the person is disqualified in that setting. They are not disqualified for life, just in that ministry. These are unfortunate situations but they do happen. The key for you as a member of a ministry is to trust the process.

You may not be exposed to all the intimate details—nor should you be! Once you see public repentance take place and a restoration process implemented, go into a time of persistent prayer. Do not hold conversations about it. Do not act as if you are the judge of the situation. Declare forgiveness over the entire matter and release it into God's hands and the oversight team. This will keep you from unproductive conversations and possibly sowing seeds of discord among the church or sowing disloyalty in your own heart.

Once a person has gone through a process of restoration and restitution, where necessary, they should know that their divine purpose has not been cancelled out. Repentance will put a person back in line and not at the back of the line. Be willing to restore someone who has fallen. When a person holds a righteous course long term, God will erase the memory of his or her past.

SECTION SIX

The Compassionate Choice - The Restoration

In 50 years of ministry, I have learned several things by experience, but I want to share both wisdom and Scriptural precedence on the topic of pastoral succession and Kingdom vision extension. A Kingdom vision is significantly different from a vision that one has that is inspired for his or her business or dreams.

A Kingdom vision has a life independent of the visionaries. When I say, "visionaries," I'm talking about all who are involved in the vision, because I'm not limiting the visionary to one person, but the group who participates in the advancement of the vision.

The church is a Kingdom vision. So, visionaries come and go, but the church stands because it is a Kingdom vision that is independent of visionaries. Throughout this book, we have talked about how to honor spiritual leadership while they are actively serving in ministry. The authenticity of the respect, recognition, and resources that we show while a person is actively serving is proven when they are no longer able to serve. Do we throw them away? Do we disregard their wishes and the vision they labored to enact by disrespecting them when they are at a vulnerable time? Let me be clear; the vision that God has given to the church is always bigger than one person. However, God gives vision to one person who is charged with implementing God's vision. God calls people to align themselves with that vision, so that it is fully resourced. In Acts chapter 16, verses 9-10, it says the following.

> "And a vision appeared to Paul in the night; there stood a man of Macedonia, and prayed him, saying, Come over into Macedonia, and help us. And after he had seen the vision, immediately we endeavored to go into Macedonia, assuredly gathering that the Lord had called us for to preach the Gospel." (Acts 16:9-10)

Here, we see that the Bible says that Paul has this vision in the night. In this vision, a man spoke to him and said, "Come over to Macedonia and help us." Then the Scripture says, "After he had seen the vision...." It is the order of God to give visions to a committed person, not a committee. The Scripture says that after he had seen the vision, "immediately we .." Only one person saw the vision, but everybody rallied around it because that's the order of God. You should never make light of a Kingdom vision.

> "Where there is no vision, the people perish: but he that keepeth the law, happy is he." (Proverbs 29:18)

Therefore, Kingdom vision delivers people from perishing predicaments.

> "And the LORD answered me, and said, Write the vision, and make it plain upon tables, that he may run that readeth it. For the vision is yet for an appointed time, but at the end it shall speak, and not lie: though it tarry, wait for it; because it will surely come, it will not tarry." (Habakkuk 2:2-3)

Here are powerful effects of walking in Kingdom vision.

First, vision rescues the perishing. If there is a Kingdom vision, it will help someone who is perishing. Look at all the lives that have been touched and transformed because of Kingdom vision.

Next, a Kingdom vision refreshes the populous. In Acts 16, do you remember what Paul said when he saw the vision and they said, "Come over and help us. Come over and refresh us?" So, beyond people being saved, a Kingdom vision refreshes people and builds them up. Whether it is through television, internet, compassion ministries to the community or supporting missionaries on foreign soil, you will see that a Kingdom Vision will build people up.

Also, a Kingdom vision reveals purpose. People throughout the Body of Christ want to know, "What is my purpose?" When one knows his or her purpose, fulfillment comes. Take for instance a chair. The chair fulfills its purpose when it holds the weight of a person in a seated position.

There is a connection between fulfillment and purpose. When a thing lives out its created purpose, fulfillment takes place, and until you live out your created purpose, you will chase what I call fulfillment decoys. That is, they told you if you had a certain kind of car, you would be fulfilled. You worked hard to purchase it and you are still empty. They told you if you lived in a certain part of town, you'd be fulfilled. You finally made it there and you are still empty. They told you if you married this type of person, you'd be in a life of bliss. You are married and still empty. It's because fulfillment is tied into created purpose.

So, if you want to know your created purpose, and if you want to be fulfilled, you cannot listen to the talk show hosts for that insight because they are not your creator. Only the creator (maker) of the thing has the right to define how the thing made ought to operate.

For us to be fulfilled, we have to know our unique purpose. Of course, we know there's a universal purpose for all of us. That's in Genesis chapter 1 when God told them to be fruitful, multiply, replenish, subdue, and have dominion. That's universal purpose. Also, there is united purpose, that which we are called to do together as a body of believers. But then, you need to know your unique purpose. In other words, "God, why am I here?"

Let me show you why a Kingdom vision is so important. You discover your unique purpose one of several ways. Ask yourself, what has God specifically said to you? And, if God hasn't said anything, don't make anything up. Believers are notorious for manufacturing revelations from God. When those things do not come true, they have to go back and create a new revelation or say that God released them.

Your purpose can also be discovered by what God is doing in your family. Because when John the Baptist was born, his purpose was already established with his mother and father, so he couldn't come on the scene and say, "I want to be a chariot mechanic," because his purpose was already established. He was going to be fulfilled being the forerunner of Jesus Christ, because that was his purpose. He could have been a chariot mechanic if he wanted to, but there would have been no fulfillment there.

So, if God hasn't said anything to me, and I don't see anything that God's doing in my family, then I get in my local church, and I put myself to work under that vision, because whatever God called them to do, I take it as if He called me to do it. (Acts 16:10) And, I will work faithfully there, until I get other directions from God.

When you are in a good church, you remain planted because your purpose is connected to that place. In the unfortunate event of a pastor's death, do not use that as an occasion to leave, unless God has specifically told you to do so. Our generation is plagued with church hoppers. God called you to a vision and if that vision is still moving forward, you should stay connected to it. You will be fulfilled in your set place because your purpose and fulfillment is linked to the Kingdom vision under which you are set.

Kingdom vision recruits its partners. When there's a Kingdom vision, people run to it and look around at what is taking place. People will always want to be a part of a Kingdom Vision. When there's a Kingdom vision, it has revolutionary potential. In other words, it does things that other people will see and be in awe. God never calls His church to do the ordinary. Kingdom vision requires the intervention of God to fulfill it. When God manifests His hand on the vision, all which see it will be amazed.

Kingdom vision requires patience. It may not happen overnight, but it will happen. Don't think that just because your church's vision has not been fully enacted that it will not be fulfilled. Remember that Kingdom vision is a marathon relay race. Also, this is why you cannot haphazardly select a successor because the new visionary has to have a respect for the vision of the previous pastor. The new pastor is just running his or her leg of a much larger race.

Because Kingdom vision is so powerful, it requires commitment from the visionaries. Remember now, when we are talking about the vision, we are not just talking about the leader, but the followers as well, because a Kingdom vision will go through seasons. Kingdom vision goes through tough times, because of the challenge of the times. The Bible says, Elijah's vision went through some tough times, because the brook at which he camped, dried up. He did not do anything wrong, it was a sign of the times. The 21st Century has started with some significant challenges, which have tried Kingdom vision. But, you cannot allow the challenge of the times to stop the progress.

Kingdom vision will also go through transitional times. It goes through transitional times because of the death, the desertion, or the dissatisfaction of key people. Now that we are talking about the key people, we are not always talking about the leader. We're talking other key people who are working.

I've been a Pastor for a long time, and there have been people in key positions who went home to be with the Lord. That area where they worked went through a transition. Transition is a part of managing vision. It is not always a transition with the spiritual leader only. It's a transition with the visionaries and people who are part of it.

Many times, people will desert you, and that is transition because of desertion. We're looking for you in Children's Ministry and you are not there. Many times, we go through transition because of people's dissatisfaction. Because your pastor cannot be at all places at all times, he or she must have help from people that can be trusted. There are people who are still growing up, and when they are dissatisfied, they will just sit down.

Kingdom vision goes through turbulent times. This is a time when we are dealing with immature people. You can understand turbulent times with teenagers and dealing with their immaturity. It's turbulent. They don't mean harm, they are just going through what I call their dumb days. And, if you have ever been in an aircraft and they had turbulence, you buckle your seat belt and you ride it out. What do you do when your teenagers are going through their dumb day? Buckle up and ride it out!

So, there are times in ministry when you will go through turbulent times and you know what to do, because turbulence doesn't last always. Now that you understand the turbulence factor, you will not abandon vision, but will buckle up and ride it out.

Thank God, Kingdom vision goes through triumphant times. When we are victorious, we use victory as a next stepping-stone that God has. Not all who are a part of the vision are operating at the level they need to be. Even in the ministry of Jesus, they saw many people around Jesus, but not everybody was His partner. Every Kingdom vision recruits and attracts its partners, and that is the difference because everybody will not be a partner.

The vision must keep moving forward even in the absence of the visionary. So, what do we do when a spiritual leader becomes incapacitated and unable to function in ministry or, worse, dies while at the helm of the ministry? How do we still display honor in those situations.

THE COMPASSIONATE RESPONSE TO DISABILITY

When I was very young in ministry, I found myself in a position where I was called in to assist a pastor who was ill and could not carry on the responsibilities of ministry. I was an associate minister at my home church, but I was sent over to help. After a long period of time, the Senior Pastor was not able to return to the pulpit. The church grew under my leadership. It had dwindled down significantly, before I assumed the reigns of the church. Week after week, the church was coming back and moving forward.

Before too long, there were people expressing their confidence in my ability to lead the church and they desired to force the Senior Pastor into retirement and make me the pastor. On the surface, everything they said was accurate. The people who were attending were coming because of my leadership and preaching. The offerings increased and the church was ready to go to the next level with me as the leader. I was seduced by the flattery and was about to make a monumental mistake.

One Sunday afternoon, and I can remember this as if it were yesterday, there was a pastor's anniversary service. It was a tradition that one of the community ministers would bring the message. Because I was the new guy in town, I knew I would be asked to preach. And, I was ready! As we talked before the service, mention was made of the job I was doing at the church and how things were going. Right when it was time to go into the service, the pastor asked that I remain back for a minute. Once everyone had left the room, he cautioned me. He affirmed that I was doing a good job and that he had heard about my progress. He then confronted me about the move that was afoot to displace the pastor and install me as the pastor. He said, "Young man, don't do it because it will break his heart." He then gave me the wisdom I shared with you earlier about making a blessing and missing a blessing.

I had a choice to make a consecrated choice! Would I feed my carnal desire to be in a charge or would I confer honor on someone at the expense of my ego? I made the right choice; I returned back to that church with a determination to let my service as interim pastor be one that glorified God and honored the work of the Senior Pastor. I squashed every movement to force the pastor into retirement and let everyone know, I served at the pleasure of that pastor.

Before too long, that pastor died with dignity and honor. Then, God opened a door for me to become the Senior Pastor in that church. However, my ascension to that position was not on the back of that previous pastor. When the transition happened, the previous pastor's family felt loved and respected and they were able to respect my leadership because I honored the one who came before me. Unfortunately, I hear stories all over the church where pastors have been disrespected when they have become incapacitated. Some have used the weakness of an ill pastor to launch a coup and steal the church from under the ailing senior pastor. The trouble with this is that it sets in motion, the law of sowing and reaping. With everyone who saw you take over that church improperly, though they may have pushed for it and encouraged it, they will know that they did something unpleasing to God. They will never respect your leadership. And, you have opened yourself up to the very real possibility that you will be displaced prematurely. It bears repeating that if you ever find yourself in a situation where you have to make a choice as to how to treat a sick pastor, always err on the side of honor! If people will conspire with you to dishonor a pastor, those same people will conspire to dishonor you! "If you make a blessing, you will miss a blessing and the blessing you miss will be greater than the blessing you made!"

You will never lose by allowing someone to finish out his ministry with dignity.

THE COURAGEOUS RESPONSE TO DEATH

The death of an active senior pastor presents a number of challenges. The key one is, How do you effectively transition the Kingdom Vision from one visionary to the next without dishonoring either person? This is where you must have a conviction in pleasing God and not people. Just like in families, a death will cause the worst to come out in people; the same is true within a church ministry.

> "When a man's ways please the LORD, he maketh even his enemies to be at peace with him."
> (Proverbs 16:7)

So, I may make some decisions that may make someone upset with me, but if I'm pleasing the Lord, by and by, even those who did not understand that I did this by the Word of God, will end up being at peace with me!

Let's gain a greater understanding about the different people in church because they will all show up upon the death of a visionary. First of all, there are parasites. Parasites are those who will take and never give back, and when you need them, they will ask you, "What have you done for me lately?" In the ministry of Jesus, there were people who were parasites. The multitudes were parasites. All they wanted was, "When are you going to feed us?" Jesus had to stop them one day and ask, "Are you only following me for the fish and the loaves?" Then, they said, "Yes!"

Then, there are players. Players are those who serve with a hidden agenda. They say, "I'm only here because I see business opportunities." Hidden agendas pollute your purpose and diminish your witness. Don't be a player. Judas was a player. Judas had a hidden agenda. When things did not go the way he intended, he turned on Jesus and became a persecutor instead of a partner.

Then, there are predators. These people have a seductive intent to exploit. Unfortunately, that's what happens when you are in transition. With everybody who comes by here, it does not mean they are well intentioned. There are predators. They will quickly arrive on the scene and try to pick people off. Remember, if your life is built upon the rock of revelation knowledge, the gates of hell cannot prevail. So, don't be concerned about the predators, because Jesus said, "Those who You put in My hand, the devil cannot pluck them out."

So, what role did the Disciples play in Jesus' ministry? You would think they were partners, but they were not. The disciples were just participators. They served with a low tolerance of discomfort. The disciples were there as long as it did not cost them anything, but when they arrested Jesus, the Bible says, they all forsook Him.

The only model we have for the partners were the women. The real partners in Jesus' ministry were the women. When He needed resources, they were there. At the cross, they were there. On resurrection morning, they were there, and that's what a real partner in ministry is about. They say, "You don't have to worry about me, I will be there. Somebody can go here or there, but I know where my real place is. I'm a real partner. You can count on me at my church. I will be there. While folk are talking or leaving, a partner will still be there.

Partners get to enjoy all the rewards of Kingdom advancement. Every victory achieved in the ministry of which you are a partner, you get credit! When you get to Heaven and the book is pulled, because you were a partner in your local church that advanced Kingdom vision, you will have confidence. You will tell them, "Go get the book."

I took the time to lay this out for you because I do not want you to be surprised when you see strange behaviors. Recognize them and be prayerful. I would be remiss if I did not explain to you the satanic corruption that comes in the succession process.

First, he tries to corrupt it with humanistic philosophy. We want to put our hands into it and try to figure it out our way.

> "Beware lest any man spoil you through philosophy and vain deceit, after the tradition of men, after the rudiments of the world, and not after Christ."
> (Colossians 2:8)

In other words, this succession process cannot be handled like the process to replace the president of a major corporation. This process cannot be handled like a traditional church that is not grounded in the Word. You cannot afford to let humanistic philosophy creep in and be the governor and guide for the process.

The succession process is corrupted by human prejudices. Human prejudice has to do with the external look and likings that we hold onto that are against what God says. Often people will try to find a successor who looks and acts just like the previous pastor. This is an unrealistic expectation.

Human passions also contaminate the process. Human passions are the feelings that you hold. Succession is not a personal endeavor. All personal preferences must be surrendered to a larger process.

Also, it is corrupted by human payoffs, which is under the table deals and human politicking. If your church has been well run and there are reserves, people will come out of the woodwork to get a piece of that vision; especially, people who themselves have not been successful.

The church is not a democracy. It is a theocracy run by God and I want to caution you not to neglect the Word! If you get off base and are not doing things God's way, you will forfeit God's assistance. In Acts chapter 16, it didn't say, after he had seen the vision, immediately they voted. In fact, we will find out that there is no voting, and it's not Biblical. You can look at any democratic system and see a level of dysfunction because in a democracy, someone wins and someone loses. In a Theocracy, God wins and the people rejoice to be a part of what He is going in their generation.

Successions are not unusual in Scripture. In fact, they give us the model for how to successfully execute a succession process. Let's look at some Scriptural case studies of succession plans because they will give you a way to understand how to manage the transition in a God-pleasing manner. All through Scripture, we can see the succession plan. The Bible gives the succession from Eli to Samuel, the succession of Moses to Joshua, the succession from Saul to David, the succession from David to Solomon, the succession from Elijah to Elisha, the succession of Jesus to the Apostles, and the succession of the Apostles to the Elders.

So, we do not have to guess how to do this, it's all in the Bible. We can't study them all, but let me give you some Scripture references. The succession plan that took place between Eli and Samuel is in I Samuel chapter 3, verses 11-18. And, in that situation, little Samuel heard from the Lord and Eli said, "What did God tell you?" And he said, "God selected me."

In the situation with Saul and David, in I Samuel chapter 16, God told the prophet, "Samuel, go down to Jesse's house. I'll show you the next king there, because I rejected Saul." So, he goes down there and Saul parades all of his fine looking boys, yet he does not hear from God. Because God said, "Man looks on the outside, but God looks at the heart."

Then he inquired and said, "Do you have any more sons?" He said, "We have one little boy out there in the pasture." Samuel said, "Go, get him." So that means God will search out the one whom He has appointed to take the vision to the next level. When David appeared before Samuel, he was anointed as King.

Then there's a succession plan between David and Solomon. God spoke to David and told him that he was not going to build the temple because he has shed too much blood as a warrior. However, God told him that Solomon would be his successor. After that, David declared it and the people accepted it." Then, we see the famous one with Elijah and Elisha.

In I Kings chapter 19, verse 15-17, God told Elijah, "Go down there and I want you to anoint this guy as king and anoint this prophet, this boy Elisha in your place." God named his successor.

When it came to Jesus, I never saw Jesus bring the multitude together and allowed them to vote, but after prayer, he choose his twelve disciples and chose his seventy. (John 20:21 and Matthew 9:10) Then, when you look at the Apostles in Acts chapter 14, verse 23, it says that they went into the cities, and based on the witness of the Spirit of God, they raised up the elders, the pastors, as it were, and they appointed them. That's the order of God.

In Numbers 27, let's look in detail into what Moses did. I think you would agree that if anyone had wisdom for leading, it was Moses. But, when it comes time for his successor, Moses does not choose his successor.

> "And Moses spoke unto the LORD, saying, Let the LORD, the God of the spirits of all flesh, set a man over the congregation."

In other words, they sought God. Moses says, "God, we need a man." Now, people were going to listen to Moses regardless. He could have just stepped out and said, "This is what we're going to do." Moses understood the sensitivity of the moment that the Kingdom vision rides on this selection.

Moses did not try to take this responsibility on his own.

> "Which may go out before them, and which may go in before them, and which may lead them out, and which may bring them in; that the congregation of the LORD be not as sheep which have no shepherd. And the LORD said unto Moses, 'Take thee Joshua the son of Nun, a man in whom is the spirit, and lay thine hand upon him; And set him before Eleazar the priest, and before all the congregation; and give him a charge in their sight. And thou shalt put some of thine honor upon him, that all the congregation of the children of Israel may be obedient. And he shall stand before Eleazar the priest, who shall ask counsel for him after the judgment of Urim before the LORD: at his word shall they go out, and at his word they shall come in, both he, and all the children of Israel with him, even all the congregation. And Moses did as the LORD commanded him: and he took Joshua, and set him before Eleazar the priest, and before all the congregation: And he laid his hands upon him, and gave him a charge, as the LORD commanded by the hand of Moses." (Numbers 27:17-23)

The people accepted God's choice without a vote. Do you see the selection process? Here's what we can draw from this Scripture. First, appointment is always by set authority. Set authority can be a prophet. Set authority can be a parent like David, or the set authority can be a panel. The principle is the set authority, which is the one who manages the transitional process. Not only the set authority, but also they must seek the Lord, get God's selection and then seek the leader.

In addition to appointment by set authority, selection can be made by a Sovereign action. Only a fool would want to be in a place where he or she is not anointed of God. You would never want someone serving in spiritual leadership without God's anointing. This is a dangerous situation, which will only decimate the Kingdom vision.

I believe this so strongly, that years ago, I was in a church and they were going through a church fight, and they put out a petition among the members to get rid of me. I took the petition and I signed my name at the top. You might say, "What? You said you signed the petition?" I say, "Yes. If all it takes to get rid of me is a piece of paper and God doesn't want me here, I'll be the first one to sign it. Give me the petition. I'll sign my name on it."

I know there are other churches around that may follow a non-Biblical approach to succession. Do not feel pressured to dismiss Scripture in favor of human tradition. If you prize the anointing, then you want to follow a path that pleases God. If not, the choice will lack the most essential element of succession– the Hand of God! When God's hand is on the ministry transition, the vision will expand, not contract.

The spiritual assembly must submit itself to the order of God. They will say, "We didn't have to vote. We prayed and followed the order of God, believing that the anointed people who were in authority would follow the dictate of the Spirit of God. When that happens, the ministry will have an anointed leader and be ready to move forward."

Why split a congregation with a vote? Why start the politicking with a vote when it's not the order of God? Now, the new man has to come in and operate in discord, because some people wanted him and others did not. But, if God's order were followed, the new person comes in without competition, confusion, and politicking, because you accept him by the Spirit of God.

Then, you will experience the advancement by supernatural assistance. God doesn't bless anything that doesn't function according to His order, and He waits for obedience before He steps in with the supernatural.

Only after you obey, do you have the justifiable right to expect a supernatural move of God. When Moses obeyed after he stretched out the rod, then the waters parted. When Joshua obeyed after he walked around the wall the seventh time, the seventh day, it was then when the walls fell down.

Naaman obeyed the instructions given to him by the Prophet, and went down into the muddy water seven times; that was when the miracle took place. Nothing happened the first, second, third, fourth, fifth or sixth time, but when he came up after obeying the seventh time, supernatural power hit his body and the leprosy left. He came up muddy, but clean, and wet, but well. (2 Kings 5)

The supernatural waits after our obedience. It was after Mary and Martha moved the stone that Jesus called their dead brother back to life. God waits for us to move. He waits to move after we have obeyed. There may be mounting pressure to follow a human path. By all means, don't do it; you will internally sabotage what God is planning for the ministry. Trust God's Word. Rely up God's succession plan.

Years ago, I bought a boat to go off shore to fish. I was an off shore fisherman. I knew nothing about boating. I grew up in the ghetto, but one of my dreams was to have a yacht. It was not a big yacht; I call it a half yacht.

It was big enough, and I hired a captain to train me so that I would not get into trouble. When you get off shore, there are no landmarks, and if you don't have landmarks, everything looks the same. So, I knew I needed some help. I hired this guy and He was there to teach me. He was teaching me everything I needed to operate the boat. He gave me one crucial piece of advice, "Now, here's the compass." I'm a boy scout and know a compass, north, south, east and west.

He said, "Ira, here's your compass. Trust your compass. No, no, no. You must listen to this. Always, trust the compass." Glibly, I said, "Yes, I understand." He said, "No, no, no, Listen; You must always trust the compass." Half convinced, I said, "I've got it." He said, "No, no, there will come a time when you are out there, and your feelings will tell you one thing, and the compass will say something else. Always, trust the compass." Thoroughly convicted, I said, "I've got it. I've got it."

True enough, I was off shore on an overcast day when I could not tell based on the sun, what was north, south, east, and west. No oilrigs were there. It had been a good day of fishing, but I needed to navigate my way home.

At the end of the day, I started to head home. Everything in me said, "You came from that direction." I checked the compass. I knew what the compass said, but everything in me knew where I came from. The wind was blowing and I thought I knew the way I came from by the way the wind blew, but the wind had shifted. I knew I came from that direction. I checked my fuel. I did not have enough fuel to make a mistake. If I headed out in the wrong direction, I was going to run out of fuel.

Then, I heard the voice of my captain saying, "When you get in a situation and your feelings are telling you one thing, and your compass says another, always trust the compass." So I pulled up anchor, started the engine, and I turned in the direction of the compass, full steam ahead. And, after about forty-five minutes, I saw Galveston Island, the compass was right.

Why am I telling you this story? I am saying that we must always trust the Word of God, for it is our compass. Whether it is to run the church, or whether it is to govern your lives, always trust the compass. God's Word will never lead you astray. God's Word will uphold the dignity and honor of His servants while they are actively serving in ministry and when a transition is made. As you have seen throughout this book, the key is that you render to God's servants what they are due, based upon God's standards, not the world's.

When we do that, we would have positioned the ministries we serve and ourselves for the supernatural!

Epilogue

This entire book has been devoted to this most important topic of honoring spiritual leadership. I could not conclude this book without making mention of how you should deal with the death of your spiritual leader.

I have already shown you the process for initiating a transition to a new generation of leadership, but I have not talked about the personal impact the death of your spiritual leader has on your life. We understand that it is inevitable that those who have poured into our lives will one day move from labor to reward.

Unfortunately, I have had the unpleasant experience of getting the heart wrenching news that a Spiritual Father and Mentor had made his transition from this life to his eternal reward. The moment you hear such news, it is as though time stands still; your mind quickly begins to catalog all the memories of past exchanges and even back to the last moment in time when you were with them. I want to close out this book by recounting for you a very personal experience that I will never forget.

When one of my spiritual leaders went home to be with the Lord, my mind raced to our last time together. It was a mutually refreshing time as I was able to share my heartfelt appreciation for all he had done for me. You see, I had never ceased to give him credit for helping me become the man I am today. To my surprise, he thanked me for all that I had done for him after reaching a level of material prosperity. (He would always mention how it made him feel special that I had not forgotten the role he played in my life.) As we shared, for what would be our last time, a pleasant smile was birthed deep inside as tears filled my eyes. It was a strange feeling: a mix of joy, but also laced with sorrow.

The days that followed hearing of his passing and leading up to the memorial service were filled with a flurry of conversations and making arrangements. The family requested that I deliver remarks at the service and I readily accepted. (It was an honor to be included.) As I meditated on what to say, I felt compelled to give my fallen hero the honor he so rightly deserved. I relished the opportunity to stand before that assembly to publicly declare my love, admiration, and appreciation for the role he played in my life. The church was filled to capacity with a standing room only crowd because many loved him. It was no secret that I was considered the favorite spiritual son and many were wondering how I would bestow honor one last time.

When the minister called my name, who was officiating the service, I approached the podium with a keen awareness of the gravity of the moment. The Holy Spirit helped me to confer honor on my spiritual mentor and to minister comfort to the family that were like my brothers and sisters. It was a moment that I will cherish forever. My honor did not end that day because I made a commitment to mention his name whenever and wherever God allowed me to go, even in circles where my spiritual mentor had never graced. I fondly and proudly inform them how his wisdom and example shaped my life. Now, why did I share all of this?

Honoring spiritual leadership is a lifelong assignment that is not based on duty, but appreciation for God using someone to bless your life. These closing words are for those who will fully embrace this Biblical concept of honoring spiritual leadership because they understand the depth of this ordained relationship. These God-sent men and women serve as living epistles for us and are the most special gifts that should always be honored as such.

Let me borrow the reflection of the Holy Spirit concerning John the Baptist as a way to reflect the totality of this ministry.

> "There was a man sent from God, whose name was John. The same came for a witness, to bear witness of the Light, that all men through him might believe. He was not that Light, but was sent to bear witness of that Light." (John 1:6-8 KJV)

Like John the Baptist, our spiritual leaders are sent from God. They are men and women sent from God; they were rescued by grace with a record of goodness and when they pass away, God receives them. We admire them because they preach with sincerity; they pray with sensitivity and they plead for souls. When we look closely, we see and know that they are not the light; Jesus is the Light and they just came to bear witness of that light.

What do you do when those who are your spiritual leaders who have been sent by God carry out their assignment and bless your life? Although we do not like to think of the times when our leaders pass off the scene, it is a reality of our existence.

The Word of God describes our Kingdom walk as warfare on this earth. In warfare, soldiers fall in battle. When they die on the battlefield, we give them a hero's send off and continue the battle with the resolve to make the enemy pay!

Relative to our spiritual leaders, we must choose to "Love Them While They Live and We Maximize the Time" they have spent with us. It is sad that most people don't realize the value of expressing their love to others, until it's too late. Be one who chooses to maximize every opportunity to express your love and appreciation to your spiritual leader.

Next, we must choose to "Loose Them When They Leave and We Will Minimize the Trauma" we can potentially experience. With those who really love Jesus, including our spiritual leaders, they long to be with the Lord. This is the teaching of the

Scripture and the sentiment of all of the apostles. Just knowing that our leaders are receiving the just reward for spending their lives serving Jesus, it is enough to loose them; otherwise, their passing can become traumatic. I have seen people resign from the faith at the death of their spiritual leaders all because they could not release their mentor who ministered to them. Your continued remembrance of their impact on your life is the way you can bring closure to their ministry.

Further, we must choose to "Learn Wisdom from Their Legacy and We Memorialize Truths" they taught us. I believe the highest honor of our spiritual leaders are shown when we implement the truths and wisdom we acquired from them. We establish their legacy as we recall what we were taught, implement the truths, and give the credit due them for their input into our lives. Quoting them and using your time of learning in illustrations keeps their memory alive. Doing so exposes them to future generations.

Finally, we must choose to "Lean Wholly on The Lord and We'll Make It Through" the difficulty of their departure. Relying on the Lord is always the key to making it through challenging times. As we rely on the Lord, we must not only rely on His strength to help us emotionally, but we must depend on this example. What did He expect from those who loved Him? It may surprise you to know that Jesus expected those who loved and honored Him to care for those of His family for whom He loved and cared.

> "Now there stood by the cross of Jesus his mother, and his mother's sister, Mary the wife of Cleophas, and Mary Magdalene. When Jesus therefore saw his mother, and the disciple standing by, whom he loved, he saith unto his mother, Woman, behold thy son! Then saith he to the disciple, Behold thy mother! And from that hour that disciple took her unto his own home." (John 19:25-27 KJV)

What did Jesus stress that His disciples should do upon His departure? Jesus stressed that they should go forth and do those things that He had taught them to do over the time of His mentorship. It is safe to conclude that we honor our spiritual leaders by living out the principles, which we were taught to the glory of God!

> "Then the eleven disciples went away into Galilee, into a mountain where Jesus had appointed them. And when they saw him, they worshipped him: but some doubted. And Jesus came and spake unto them, saying, All power is given unto me in heaven and in earth. Go ye therefore, and teach all nations, baptizing them in the name of the Father, and of the Son, and of the Holy Ghost: Teaching them to observe all things whatsoever I have commanded you: and, lo, I am with you alway, even unto the end of the world. Amen." (Matthew 28:16-20 KJV)

As you can deduce from all that I have presented, honoring spiritual leadership is a lifelong commitment because God in His

Infinite Wisdom has appointed people to help you achieve your destiny. You demonstrate your appreciation to God by honoring those whom He has sent. When you do this, you release a supernatural grace on your life to achieve at a higher level and live a first-class lifestyle. Please don't let this be just a book! I wrote this from my heart to encourage you to embrace a Scriptural principle that has transformed my life. I am certain it will have the same effect on your life. Don't delay to implement this truth and you will see the supernatural hand of God move in your life in amazing ways. I can't wait to hear your testimony!

52 DAYS CAN CHANGE YOUR LIFE

Problems are common in life, but only *maximizers* solve those problems! Become a *maximizer* and change your life in just 52 days. Life coach and teacher, I.V. Hilliard, has written **The Maximized Life Journey** to daily encourage you in your walk of faith. The wisdom shared in this book has changed thousands of lives; let it change yours today!

The Maximized Life Journey
A 52-DAY DEVOTIONAL THAT WILL REBUILD YOUR LIFE!

Call 1-855-97-LIGHT (54448) -or-
scan the QR Code to the right to purchase and find out more about this product!

THE MOST-INTERACTIVE TEXTBOOK EVER PRESENTED

USE THIS TOOL TO GAIN:
- A Better Understanding of Kingdom Economics
- Practical Strategies to Develop Financial Strength
- Strategies for Solving Financial Difficulties
- Concepts for Creative Financial Increase

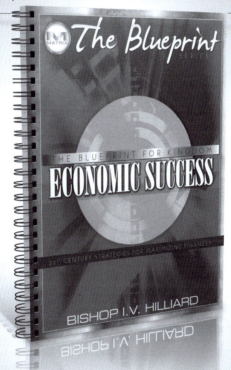

The Blueprint for Kingdom Economic Success

AS YOU READ YOU WILL BE ABLE TO CONNECT WITH VIDEO SEMINARS, AUDIO FILES, & SUPPLEMENTARY RESOURCES THAT WILL COMPLETE THE LEARNING EXPERIENCE.

Call 1-855-97-LIGHT (54448) -or- scan the QR Code to the right to purchase and find out more about this product!

Your most urgent need from God is very important to me!

You are so important to God! I want to help you by building your faith. I want to hear from you when you are facing a spiritual need or experiencing hardships in your life. Write me. I will pray with you and write you back with faith-builidng principles to get you the answers you need!

PLEASE PRINT YOUR PRAYER REQUEST BELOW

_____

_____

_____

_____

_____

_____

_____

NAME _____

ADDRESS _____

CITY _____ STATE _____ ZIP _____

PHONE _____ BIRTHDATE __/__/__

CLIP & MAIL TO:
Bishop I.V. Hilliard
P.O. Box 670167
Houston, TX 77267

or scan the QR Code to the left on your smartphone to submit your prayer request online and receive faith-building letters from Bishop Hilliard.